# Italian Easy: Recipes from the London River Cafe
## Rose Gray and Ruth Rogers

CLARKSON POTTER / PUBLISHERS
NEW YORK

Photography by Martyn Thompson   Design by the Senate

*Frozen Sculpture by Marc Quinn*

# Contents

The Italian food in this book is easy to cook. Each recipe emphasizes the things we value at the River Cafe – freshness, subtlety and quality – while being short, easy to shop for, and easy to serve.

Simple, delicious food relies on its ingredients. Here you'll find a useful guide of what to keep in your cupboards and in your refrigerator: olive oil, capers, balsamic vinegar, organic eggs, pancetta, and more. Each recipe begins with a shopping list to make it easier to buy the things you'll need, and we've shown you where shortcuts can be taken.

We want you to feel inspired and confident in cooking Italian food. In chapters such as Tutti Ricotta, we give many ways to use one basic ingredient. The pastas are divided into Spaghetti, Short Pasta, and Tagliatelle to show how in Italian cooking each suggests a different type of sauce. You'll see that Gnocchi needn't be as hard to make as you think, and that Carpaccio can mean beef or fish. Most of the recipes serve four and many are very quick to prepare, including a 15-minute Chocolate Cake.

Where we think it will be helpful, we have added notes on ingredients, methods, and equipment. There is a Sauces and Basics section at the end of the book that provides you with the fundamentals of Italian cooking – like peeling tomatoes and preparing salted anchovies – and recipes for the sauces we use most. We have included a list of suppliers, though most of the ingredients are widely available.

Easy food doesn't have to mean unsophisticated food. Although the cookbook concentrates on simplicity, there's always some surprise element, some little twist that comes from what we've learned over the years, both at the River Cafe and when cooking with Italians in their kitchens. We hope you take as much pleasure in cooking these easy recipes as we do.

**Rose Gray & Ruth Rogers**, London 2004

**1** Basic
bruschetta

**2** Asparagus
Parmesan

**3** Asparagus
prosciutto

**4** Tomato
borlotti

**5** Broccoli
olives

**6** Roasted
zucchini

**7** Fennel
olives

**8** Fig
arugula

**9** Prosciutto
spinach

**10** Mozzarella
olives

**11** Mozzarella
chiles

**12** Borlotti
prosciutto

**13**
Fennel
prosciutto

**14**
Cavolo nero
prosciutto

**15**
Tomato
prosciutto

**16**
Chickpea
Swiss chard

**17**
Ricotta
red chiles

**18**
Tomato
olives

**19**
Fava bean
pecorino

**20**
Mozzarella
anchovies

**21**
Crab
lemon

**22**
Mozzarella
tomato

**23**
Chickpea
tomato

**24**
Grilled
eggplant

**Bruschetta**

## 1 Basic bruschetta

Grill a generous piece of sourdough bread on both sides. Lightly rub one side with peeled garlic, season, and pour over olive oil.

## 2 Asparagus Parmesan

Boil the asparagus until tender. While still warm, season and toss with olive oil and lemon. Add arugula, toss and then put on bruschetta with Parmesan shavings.

## 3 Asparagus prosciutto

Boil the asparagus until tender. While still warm, season and toss with olive oil and red wine vinegar. Add arugula, toss and then put on bruschetta with slices of prosciutto.

## 4 Tomato borlotti

Toss cherry tomatoes with olive oil and pieces of peeled garlic and season. Roast in a 400°F oven for 15 minutes. Season warm borlotti beans and mix with olive oil and red wine vinegar. Combine with tomatoes. Place on bruschetta with an anchovy fillet.

## 5 Broccoli olives

Boil purple-sprouting broccoli until tender. Season and toss with olive oil and lemon. Put on bruschetta with pitted black olives and toasted pine nuts.

## 6 Roasted zucchini

Cut zucchini lengthwise into $1/_4$-inch slices. Place in a roasting pan, season, drizzle with olive oil and bake in a 400°F oven until just crisp. Put on bruschetta with chopped large fresh red chiles and mint, and drizzle with olive oil.

## 7 Fennel olives

Slice fennel bulb lengthwise into
$3/_4$-inch pieces and boil until tender.
Season and toss with olive oil and
lemon. Add arugula and then put on
bruschetta with chopped large fresh
red chiles and pitted black olives.

## 8 Fig arugula

Cut figs into quarters or eighths,
depending on size. Season and toss
with olive oil and balsamic vinegar.
Add arugula, put on bruschetta and
drizzle with olive oil.

## 9 Prosciutto spinach

Boil spinach until tender. Drain and
press out the water. Season and toss
with a generous amount of olive oil.
Put on bruschetta with slices of
prosciutto.

## 10 Mozzarella olives

Cut mozzarella into $1/_2$-inch slices.
Toss arugula with olive oil and
lemon juice, and season. Put on
bruschetta with pitted black olives,
mozzarella, and marjoram. Sprinkle
pepper over the mozzarella and
drizzle with olive oil.

## 11 Mozzarella chiles

Cut mozzarella into $1/_2$-inch slices.
Toss arugula in olive oil and lemon
juice, and season. Put on bruschetta
with mozzarella, large fresh red
chiles and pepper. Drizzle with
olive oil.

## 12 Borlotti prosciutto

Combine the warm borlotti beans
with red wine vinegar and olive oil,
and season. Place on bruschetta
with slices of prosciutto. Drizzle with
olive oil.

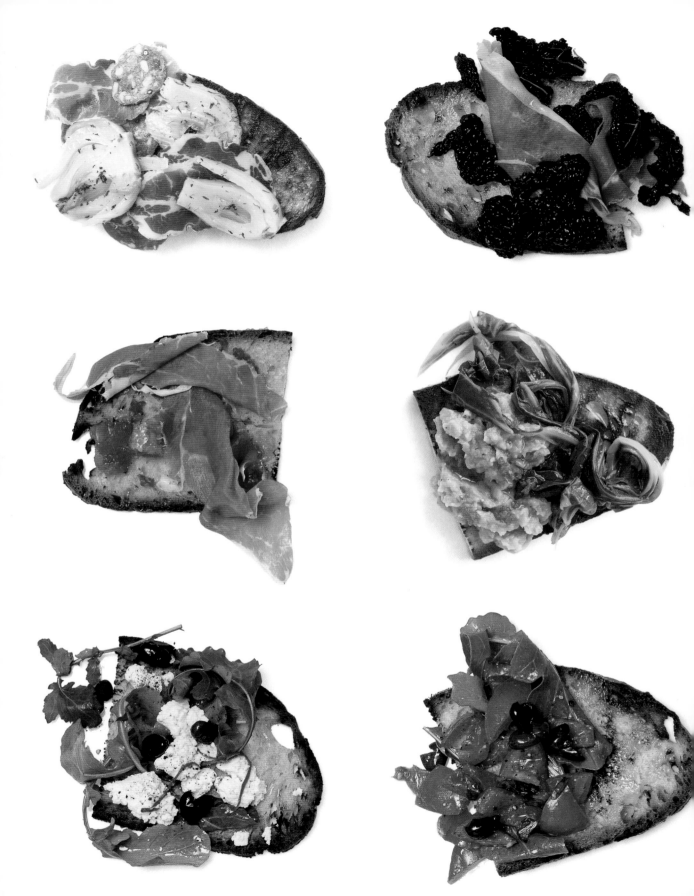

## 13  Fennel prosciutto

Slice the fennel lengthwise into $1/2$-inch pieces. Reserve the leafy tops. Boil the pieces until tender. Toss while warm with olive oil and lemon juice, and season. Put on bruschetta with salami and prosciutto, and scatter with the leafy fennel tops.

## 14  Cavolo nero prosciutto

Remove stems from the tender leaves of cavolo nero (black Tuscan cabbage) and boil leaves until soft. Drain, season and toss with olive oil. Place on a bruschetta with slices of prosciutto. Serve while the cavolo is warm.

## 15  Tomato prosciutto

Cut a ripe large tomato in half and press the cut side onto bruschetta, squeezing the pulp and the juice into the bread. Rub with peeled garlic. Season and drizzle over olive oil. Serve with slices of prosciutto.

## 16  Chickpea Swiss chard

Boil the chard leaves until tender, drain well, and roughly chop. Sauté in olive oil with garlic and season. Rinse chickpeas and briefly heat with olive oil and the juice of a lemon. Season and puree. Place puree and chard on bruschetta. Spoon over chopped red chile. Drizzle with olive oil.

## 17  Ricotta red chiles

Broil whole red chiles. Place in a bowl and cover with plastic wrap. When cool, remove skins and seeds. Cover with olive oil. Toss with arugula. Season with lemon juice and olive oil. Put on bruschetta with slices of ricotta, red chile, and pitted black olives.

## 18  Tomato olives

Cut plum tomatoes in half and squeeze out seeds and juices. Toss the flesh with olive oil, red wine vinegar, and dried chiles. Season and then place on bruschetta with arugula and pitted black olives. Drizzle with olive oil.

## 19 Fava bean pecorino

Boil fava beans until tender. Drain and season, adding olive oil, lemon juice, and fresh mint leaves. Put on bruschetta with shavings of fresh pecorino.

## 20 Mozzarella anchovies

Marinate rinsed salted anchovies in olive oil and lemon juice. Cut the mozzarella into $1/2$-inch slices. Toss arugula with olive oil and lemon juice and put on bruschetta with the anchovies and mozzarella slices. Season with black pepper and drizzle with olive oil.

## 21 Crab lemon

Mix white crabmeat with lemon juice, olive oil, dried chiles, and crushed fennel seeds, and season. Toss salad leaves with lemon juice and olive oil and place with the crab on bruschetta. Drizzle with olive oil.

## 22 Mozzarella tomato

Toss cherry tomatoes with olive oil and pieces of peeled garlic. Season and roast in a 400°F oven for 15 minutes. Slice mozzarella into $1/2$-inch pieces. Toss arugula leaves with olive oil and lemon, place on bruschetta with tomatoes and slices of mozzarella. Drizzle with olive oil.

## 23 Chickpea tomato

Toss cherry tomatoes, olive oil, pieces of peeled garlic and rosemary. Season and roast in a 400°F oven for 15 minutes. Rinse the canned chickpeas and heat with olive oil and dried chiles, and season. Add to tomatoes. Rub bruschetta with fresh rosemary and spoon over chickpeas and tomatoes. Drizzle with olive oil.

## 24 Grilled eggplant

Cut eggplants into very thin slices and grill on both sides. Toss with olive oil and lemon juice, and season. Add sliced basil and place on bruschetta with chopped large fresh red chiles. Drizzle with olive oil.

# Bruschetta

In its simplest form, bruschetta is grilled bread rubbed with garlic and drizzled with extra virgin olive oil. To make good bruschetta, you need bread that has a firm crumb, open texture, and a crisp crust. When possible, choose a sourdough loaf, with a strong flavor that varies with the type of flour used.

The quality of the oil is equally important. The River Cafe bottles four single-estate, cold-pressed Tuscan olive oils made from different varieties of olive, each with a distinctive character. We look for the freshest, greenest, most peppery oils. Pressed at the end of October, the oil is spiciest in the first few months, and more mellow later in the year, when it is also good for use in salads. Our olive oils are Selvapiana from Chianti Rufina, Morello from just north of Florence, Capezzana from Carmignano, and I Canonici from Polvereto.

# 1
Bread and tomato

# 2
Mozzarella and red pepper

# 3
Potato and parsley

# 4
Lentil and ricotta

# 5
Green bean and anchovy

# 6
Asparagus and anchovy

# 7
Porcini and Parmesan

# 8
Summer leaves

# 9
Mixed winter leaves

# 10
Puntarelle alla Romana

# 11
Crab and fennel salad

# 12
Toasted ciabatta salad

# 13
Roasted beets

# 14
Raw fennel and Parmesan

# 15
Fresh borlotti bean salad

# Antipasti

# 1

# Bread and tomato

| | |
|---|---|
| Sourdough loaf | 1/2 |
| Plum tomatoes | 6 |
| Cherry tomatoes | 10 |
| Red wine vinegar | 2 tbsp |
| Ex.v.olive oil | 5 tbsp |
| Basil leaves | 4 tbsp |

Peel the plum tomatoes (see page 260), put in a food processor, and puree until smooth. Add the red wine vinegar and 2 tbsp of the olive oil and season.

Crumble the stale bread in a bowl, add the pureed tomatoes and mix, using your hands, until totally combined.

Cut the cherry tomatoes in half, squeeze out the seeds and juice, then season and add the flesh to the bread mixture along with the basil.

Drizzle over the remaining olive oil.

Sourdough bread makes the best bruschetta and bread crumbs. A loaf will last 3-4 days, and a stale one is best for bread crumbs. If the bread is fresh, roughly tear it up and bake in a low oven to dry for 30 minutes before crumbling.

# 2

# Mozzarella and red pepper

| | |
|---|---|
| Buffalo mozzarella | 2 |
| Red bell peppers | 2 |
| Cherry tomatoes | 10 |
| Ex.v.olive oil | 4 tbsp |
| Plum tomatoes | 4 |
| Red wine vinegar | 1 tbsp |
| Basil leaves | 4 tbsp |

Heat the oven to 400°F, and heat the grill or a grill pan.

Toss the cherry tomatoes with 1 tbsp of olive oil, season, and roast for 15 minutes.

Grill the peppers until black. Put in a plastic bag until cool, then remove the skins, core, and seeds. Tear lengthwise into quarters. Slice the mozzarella.

Cut the plum tomatoes in half and squeeze out the seeds and juice. Cut each half in half.

Mix together the vinegar and remaining olive oil, season, and pour over the plum tomatoes and pepper. Add the cherry tomatoes and the basil. Serve with the mozzarella.

# 3

# Potato and parsley

| Waxy potatoes | 2 lbs |
| Red wine vinegar | 3 tbsp |
| Ex.v.olive oil | 4 tbsp |
| Garlic clove | 1 |
| Parsley leaves | 3 tbsp |

Peel and boil the potatoes in salted water until tender. Drain and, while still warm, slice 1/2 inch thick. Carefully place onto a flat plate. Drizzle with the vinegar and olive oil, and season. Peel and chop the garlic and chop the parsley. Scatter both over the potatoes. Drizzle with more olive oil.

# 4

# Lentil and ricotta

| Lentils | 1 cup |
| Ricotta | 1 cup |
| Garlic clove | 1 |
| Red wine vinegar | 1 tbsp |
| Parsley leaves | 2 tbsp |
| Basil leaves | 2 tbsp |
| Arugula leaves | 2 tbsp |
| Ex.v.olive oil | |

Rinse the lentils. Put into a thick-bottomed pan with the peeled garlic and cover with water. Bring to a boil and simmer for about 20 minutes. Drain and remove the garlic. Add 3 tbsp olive oil and the vinegar. Season while still warm.

Chop the herbs and arugula and stir into the lentils to combine the flavors.

Turn the ricotta out carefully. Slice thinly and place over the lentils. Season and drizzle with olive oil.

Use a wet ricotta rather than a crumbly one, as it will slice more easily. Castelluccio (Italian) and Puy (French) lentils cook quickly, have distinctive nutty flavors, and are equally delicious warm or cold.

# 5

# Green bean and anchovy

| | |
|---|---|
| Green beans | 2 lbs |
| Anchovy fillets | 10 |
| Ex.v.olive oil | 4 tbsp |
| Capers | 2 tbsp |
| Lemon | 1 |
| Niçoise olives | 4 oz |
| Basil leaves | 2 tbsp |

Boil the beans in salted water until soft. Drain, then season and toss with 2 tbsp olive oil.

Chop the rinsed anchovies and capers together, put into a bowl, and stir in lemon juice to combine. Add 2 tbsp olive oil and stir.

Pit the olives and tear the basil. Mix the beans into the sauce. Scatter over olives and basil.

Anchovies preserved in salt and then rinsed will "melt" much more effectively than anchovies preserved in oil because the oil acts as a barrier (see page 260).

**6**

# Asparagus and anchovy

Asparagus             2 lbs
Anchovy fillets          6
Unsalted butter  1¼ sticks
Lemon                   ½
Parmesan              2 oz
Ex.v.olive oil

Soften the butter. Rinse, dry, and roughly chop the anchovies.

In a bowl, mix the anchovies with lemon juice and black pepper, then use a fork to mix with the butter.

Boil the asparagus in salted water until tender. Drain, season, and drizzle with olive oil.

Place the asparagus on warm plates. Spoon over the anchovy butter, and scatter with Parmesan shavings.

Choose asparagus with tightly closed tips and firm stems. Asparagus steamers are designed to protect the fragile tips because they cook the stems standing upright. Alternatively, lay the asparagus flat in a large skillet and cover with boiling salted water.

# 7

# Porcini and Parmesan

| | |
|---|---|
| Fresh porcini | 1 lb |
| Parmesan | 2 oz |
| Parsley leaves | 2 tbsp |
| Dried chile | 1 |
| Lemon | 1 |
| Ex.v.olive oil | |

Cut thin slices of the porcini lengthwise through the stem. Finely chop the parsley and crumble the chile.

Mix the parsley with the juice of $1/2$ lemon and 2 tbsp olive oil. Season.

Place the porcini slices over each plate. Scatter with chile, and season. Squeeze over the remainder of the lemon juice. Scatter the parsley and cover with Parmesan shavings. Drizzle with olive oil.

Look for medium-size, firm, fresh porcini for this salad, and trim away the earthy bits at the base. Peel the stem, but do not detach from the cap. Wipe the caps with a damp cloth.

# 8

# Summer leaves

| | |
|---|---|
| Mixed leaves | 9 oz |
| Black olives | 2 tbsp |
| Marjoram leaves | 2 tbsp |
| Garlic clove | 1 |
| Red wine vinegar | 1 tbsp |
| Ex.v.olive oil | 3 tbsp |
| Lemon | 1/2 |
| Pecorino staginata | 7 oz |

Wash the leaves and spin dry. Pit the olives, chop the marjoram, peel and chop the garlic, and mix these in a bowl with the vinegar and 2 tbsp olive oil. Season.

Stir together the lemon juice and remaining olive oil and season. Pour over the leaves and toss. Spoon over the olives and cover with pecorino shavings.

Summer leaf salad can include the cucumber-flavored purslane, available in Greek, Turkish and Lebanese stores; nasturtium leaves; the small leaves from fresh beets; spinach; sorrel; and Swiss chard. Orache is an unusual Mediterranean plant with a metallic flavor – pick the small red leaves before the plant flowers. Certain edible flowers are also delicious: white cultivated arugula flowers are peppery, while zucchini flowers add color. Fresh summer herbs, such as basil, mint and marjoram, used sparingly, are an interesting addition. Pecorino staginata is the hard, aged Tuscan pecorino.

# 9

# Mixed winter leaves

| | |
|---|---|
| Mixed leaves | 9 oz |
| Balsamic vinegar | 2 tbsp |
| Ex.v.olive oil | 5 tbsp |

Wash the leaves and spin dry.

Stir together the vinegar and olive oil and season. Pour over the leaves, and toss to coat each leaf.

To make a winter salad interesting, use bitter leaves, such as cultivated dandelion, cicoria, trevise, radicchio, and red and white endive. Lemony sorrel, peppery arugula, hot mustard leaf, metallic spinach and fresh mâche are in season, too. You could also include winter herbs, such as mint, flat-leaf parsley, the pale yellow center leaves of celery, and the green tips of Florence fennel.

# 10

# Puntarelle alla Romana

| | |
|---|---|
| Puntarelle heads | 2 |
| Salted anchovies | 5 |
| Red wine vinegar | 2 tbsp |
| Garlic clove | 1 |
| Dried chiles | 2 |
| Black pepper | 1 tsp |
| Ex.v.olive oil | 4 tbsp |
| Lemon | 1 |

To prepare puntarelle, fill a bowl with cold water and ice cubes. Pull the hollow buds from the puntarelle heads. Using a small knife, slice the buds very thinly lengthwise. Place in the water to crisp and curl up. This will take an hour.

Rinse and fillet the anchovies (see page 260), cut into 1/2-inch pieces, and place in a small bowl. Cover with the vinegar, and stir to let the anchovy dissolve. Peel and chop the garlic very finely and add to the anchovies with the crumbled chiles and pepper. Leave for 15 minutes, and then add the olive oil.

Spin-dry the puntarelle as for a salad. Place in a bowl and spoon over the anchovy sauce. Serve with lemon.

This unusual salad is traditionally Roman. Puntarelle, also called catalogna, is a slightly bitter Italian vegetable that is available from specialist suppliers at certain times of the year. The season starts in November and ends in February (see suppliers' list, page 263). If you can't find any, substitute sliced red chicory.

# 11

# Crab and fennel salad

| | |
|---|---|
| Crab cooked in shell | 4½ lbs |
| Fennel bulbs | 2 |
| Lemons | 1½ |
| Dried chile | 1 |
| Parsley leaves | 1 tbsp |
| Ex.v. olive oil | |

For the fennel salad, cut off the leafy tops. Cut the fennel across into ¼-inch slices to make rings. Heat the broiler and broil the fennel on both sides until lightly charred. Season and toss with 2 tbsp olive oil and the juice of ½ lemon.

Crumble the chile and finely chop the parsley and fennel tops.

For the crab, pick the white and brown meats out of the shell, keeping them separate. Stir the chile, parsley, and fennel tops into the white meat. Season and add 1 tbsp lemon juice and 2 tbsp olive oil.

Season the brown meat. Serve the crabmeats with the fennel salad, drizzle with olive oil, and serve with lemon.

For crab salad you need freshly picked crab. Choose a cooked crab that smells fresh and has its legs drawn up into the body. This indicates the crab was alive when cooked and it will taste sweet and delicious. Picking crab does take time and is a task best shared.

# 12

# Toasted ciabatta salad

| | |
|---|---|
| Ciabatta loaf | 1 |
| Tomatoes | 1 1/2 lbs |
| Capers | 4 tbsp |
| Garlic clove | 1 |
| Red wine vinegar | 2 tbsp |
| Anchovy fillets | 8 |
| Basil leaves | 3 tbsp |
| Ex.v.olive oil | |

Heat the oven to 400°F.

Peel the tomatoes (see page 260) and cut each in half. Over a strainer, spoon out the fleshy insides and push as much of the juice through as you can. Put the tomato halves in a bowl with the rinsed capers and season.

Crush the peeled garlic with 1 tsp salt. Stir into the juice. Add the vinegar and 5 tbsp olive oil, and season.

Trim the crust off the bottom of the bread. Tear into thin, leaflike pieces, season and place on a cookie sheet. Drizzle with olive oil and bake in the oven until light brown and crunchy. Put the hot bread pieces in a large bowl. Pour over the juice and add a little more olive oil. Mix in the tomatoes, and add the anchovies and basil. Serve warm.

Mix a variety of tomatoes, such as yellow marigold, fleshy oxheart and cherry vine, to make this salad more unusual.

# 13

# Roasted beets

| | |
|---|---|
| Beets | 14 |
| Garlic cloves | 2 |
| Thyme leaves | 2 tbsp |
| Arugula leaves | 4 oz |
| Red wine vinegar | 3 tbsp |
| Horseradish root | 4 oz |
| Ex.v.olive oil | |

Heat the oven to 400°F.

Cut the peeled garlic in half. Cut the leaves 3/4 inch from the beets (keep to use in a salad). Scrub the beets thoroughly, then place in a roasting pan. Season generously, scatter with thyme and garlic, and drizzle with olive oil.

Cover loosely with foil and bake in the oven for 20 minutes. Remove the foil, turn the beets round in the olive oil, and continue roasting for 30 minutes longer.

Cut the beets in half and arrange on plates. Place the arugula among them. Season, and drizzle with 4 tbsp olive oil and vinegar. Grate over the fresh horseradish.

Buy beets sold with their leaves attached, root tail intact, and golfball size. Look for different varieties. Golden beets are a rich, deep yellow and very sweet. There is also a striped variety, and a long, oval variety that is deep red and has a strong beet flavor. Horseradish has always been grown in traditional vegetable gardens, and also grows wild in many places. The plant is cultivated for the root, which needs to be peeled before being grated on the finest part of the grater.

# 14 Raw fennel and Parmesan

| | |
|---|---|
| Fennel bulbs | 3 |
| Parmesan | 2 oz |
| Lemon juice | 3 tbsp |
| Ex.v.olive oil | 4 tbsp |
| Prosciutto slices | 12 |

Trim the fennel. Chop the leafy tops.

Slice the bulbs lengthwise very thinly and toss together with the lemon juice and olive oil, then season. Shave the Parmesan and combine. Leave to marinate for 1 hour, tossing occasionally. Before serving, add the fennel tops. Serve with prosciutto or salami.

# 15 Fresh borlotti bean salad

| | |
|---|---|
| Fresh borlotti beans | 2½ lbs |
| Garlic cloves | 2 |
| Sage leaves | 3 tbsp |
| Red wine vinegar | 1 tbsp |
| French mustard | 2 tbsp |
| Ex.v.olive oil | 5 tbsp |
| Arugula leaves | 9 oz |

Pod the beans and cover with cold water. Add the peeled garlic and sage leaves. Bring to a boil, and simmer for 35 minutes until soft. Drain and season.

Combine the vinegar and mustard, and season. Slowly add the olive oil.

Toss the beans with two-thirds of the dressing. Toss the arugula leaves in the remainder of the dressing.

Divide the dressed leaves between the plates. Spoon the beans over the leaves, and serve with the bean juices over.

Fresh borlotti (also known as cranberry beans) are magenta and white both inside and out. The season for these beans is summer.

**1** Beef
carpaccio

**2** Sea bass
carpaccio

**3** Tuna
carpaccio

**4** Marinated
anchovies

**5** Beef tenderloin
with thyme

# Carpaccio

# 1

# Beef carpaccio

| Beef tenderloin | 1½ lbs |
| Ex.v.olive oil | 1½ cups |
| Pine nuts | ½ cup |
| Parmesan | 4 oz |
| Lemons | 2 |

Cut the tenderloin at a slight angle into 3/4-inch slices. Lay each slice on plastic wrap, and cover with another piece of plastic wrap. Pound flat to extend and thin out each slice.

Pour in olive oil to cover the bottom of a dish that will hold the beef slices in 2 layers. Season the beef generously on both sides, and arrange a layer in the dish. Pour over more olive oil, and repeat with another layer of beef. The slices should be submerged. Cover with plastic wrap and place in the refrigerator for 30 minutes.

Lightly toast the pine nuts over a gentle heat in a dry skillet. Shave the Parmesan into slivers.

To serve, lift the beef slices from the marinade and put on a plate. Scatter with the pine nuts and the Parmesan. Serve with lemon.

This unusual version of carpaccio comes from Verona and is often served with Broiled radicchio (see page 210). Ask for short tenderloin, the fine-grained center cut, otherwise known as the chateaubriand.

# 2

# Sea bass carpaccio

| | |
|---|---|
| Sea bass | 4 lb |
| Cherry tomatoes | 8 |
| Lemons | 2 |
| Dried chiles | 3 |
| Ex.v.olive oil | 3 tbsp |
| Marjoram leaves | 3 tbsp |

Place the bass fillets skin side down on a board. Using a long-bladed knife, cut the slices as finely as you can along the whole length of the fillet. Place the slices side by side on cold plates.

Squeeze the juices and a little pulp out of the tomatoes over the bass. The tomato acids will slightly "cook" the fish. Drizzle with lemon juice, season, and add a few flakes of chile. Finally pour over 3 tbsp olive oil and scatter with a few marjoram leaves. Serve with lemon.

Ask the fish merchant to clean, scale, and cut the fish into 2 fillets. The fillet cut from a large sea bass weighing around 4 lbs is the easiest to slice finely. Sea bass for carpaccio should always be very fresh. Medium to large line-caught wild fish will always have the best flavor.

# 3

# Tuna carpaccio

| | |
|---|---:|
| Tuna loin | 1$\frac{1}{2}$ lbs |
| Capers | 1 oz |
| Lemons | 3 |
| Arugula leaves | 4 oz |
| Ex.v.olive oil | |

To make the slicing easier, wrap the piece of tuna tightly in plastic wrap and place in the freezer for 2 hours to firm up.

Marinate the rinsed capers for 30 minutes in the juice of $\frac{1}{2}$ lemon and enough olive oil to cover.

Use a long-bladed knife to cut the tuna across the grain as thinly as you possibly can.

Arrange the slices on cold plates, and season. Scatter over the capers and the arugula, and drizzle with the juice of a whole lemon and olive oil. Serve with lemon.

Small, spiky-leafed wild arugula, known as Capri arugula or Turkish arugula, is best for this recipe, as its hot, peppery taste contrasts with the oily richness of the tuna. Salted capers have a fresher taste than those preserved in vinegar. Wash off the salt before marinating.

# 4

# Marinated anchovies

| | |
|---|---|
| Fresh anchovies | 1 1/2 lbs |
| Rosemary sprig | 1 |
| Fennel seeds | 1 tsp |
| Dried chile | 1 |
| Lemons | 2 |
| Red wine vinegar | 3 tbsp |
| Ex.v.olive oil | |

To fillet the anchovies, pull the head and spine away from the fish, then pull off the tails and fins to make 2 fillets. Rinse and lay out on paper towels.

Chop the rosemary finely and mix immediately with 1 tbsp salt. Grind the fennel seeds and crumble the chile.

Scatter some of the rosemary, fennel, chile, and black pepper over the surface of a serving dish. Drizzle with lemon juice and olive oil.

Place the anchovies skin side up in the dish, packing them closely together. Sprinkle them with rosemary, fennel, chile, black pepper, lemon, vinegar, and olive oil. Make additional layers, repeating the process. Make sure the final layer is submerged.

Cover with plastic wrap and leave to "cook" in the marinade for at least an hour.

Fresh anchovies marinated in this way will keep for up to 2 days in a refrigerator. They are delicious served with bruschetta and a mixed-leaf salad.

# 5

# Beef tenderloin with thyme

| | |
|---|---|
| Beef tenderloin | 1½ lbs |
| Black peppercorns | 2 tbsp |
| Thyme leaves | 3 tbsp |
| Lemons | 3 |
| Parmesan | 4 oz |
| Wild arugula leaves | 4 oz |
| Ex.v.olive oil | |

Grind the peppercorns and mix with ½ tbsp salt and the thyme.

Rub the tenderloin lightly with olive oil, then rub the pepper mixture into the beef. Heat a grill pan to very hot, and sear the beef on all sides. Cool.

Use a long, sharp-bladed knife to slice the beef as thinly as possible. Place the slices on a board and press with the flat blade of the knife to extend each slice.

Cover a cold plate with the beef. Season and drizzle over the juice of ½ lemon.

Shave the Parmesan. Toss the arugula with olive oil and a little more lemon juice. Scatter the leaves over the beef, then put the Parmesan shavings on top. Drizzle over more olive oil and serve with lemon.

**1**
Fava
bean

**2**
Pappa
pomodoro

**3**
Cavolo
nero

**4**
Pea, pancetta,
and zucchini

**5**
Artichoke and
potato

**6**
Rice and
potato

**7**
Clam and
fennel

**8**
Zucchini and
cannellini

**9**
Pumpkin
crostini

**10**
Quick
fish

**11**
Chickpea and
shrimp

**Soup**

# 1

# Fava bean

| | |
|---|---|
| Podded fava beans | 2 cups |
| Podded peas | 2 cups |
| Garlic cloves | 2 |
| Waxy potatoes | 1 lb |
| Chicken stock | 1¼ cups |
| Basil leaves | 4 tbsp |
| Sourdough loaf | ¼ |
| Ex.v.olive oil | |

Peel and chop the garlic. Peel and cut the potatoes into 3/4-inch cubes.

Heat 2 tbsp olive oil in a thick-bottomed pan and fry the garlic until soft. Add the potato, stir and season, then add the fava beans, peas, and stock. Cook for 15 minutes until the potatoes are soft. Place half the soup in a food processor and roughly pulse, then return to the same pan. Add the basil. The soup should be thick.

Heat the oven to 400°F. Thickly slice the bread, trim the crusts, and tear into pieces. Drizzle with olive oil. Season and bake until lightly toasted.

Put the bread in the bowls. Spoon the soup over and drizzle with olive oil.

This very thick soup of fava beans and potatoes requires very little stock, as the flavor is in the beans and basil. It is fine to use a quality bought chicken stock in this recipe.

# 2

# Pappa pomodoro

| | |
|---|---|
| Can tomatoes | 28 oz |
| Garlic cloves | 2 |
| Sourdough loaf | 1/4 |
| Chicken stock | 1 cup |
| Sage leaves | 2 tbsp |
| Ex.v.olive oil | |

Peel and slice the garlic. Slice the bread into 1/2-inch slices.

Heat a thick-bottomed pan. Add the stock and 6 tbsp olive oil, the sage, and the garlic. When the stock begins to evaporate and the garlic starts to color, add the bread. "Fry" over high heat until the stock is absorbed and the bread is crisp.

Add the tomatoes and season. Stir to break up the bread and cook for 15 minutes. Pour over enough water to loosen the soup. It should be a thick consistency. Cook for 5 minutes longer.

Serve with more olive oil.

The flavor of this thick soup comes from "frying" the bread in the stock and olive oil before adding the tomatoes. It is fine to use a quality bought chicken stock. In the summer make the soup with 18 oz of peeled and seeded fresh tomatoes.

# 3

# Cavolo nero

Cavolo nero          1 1/2 lbs
Garlic cloves               4
Red onions                  2
Carrots                     4
Celery head                 1
Dried chile                 1
Can borlotti beans      14 oz
Fennel seeds          1/2 tsp
Can tomatoes     1/2 x 14 oz
Chicken stock     2 1/4 cups
Sourdough loaf            1/4
Ex.v.olive oil

Peel the garlic, onions, and carrots. Roughly chop 3 garlic cloves, the onions, pale celery heart, and carrots. Crumble the chile. Drain and rinse the beans.

Heat 3 tbsp olive oil in a thick-bottomed pan, add the onion, celery, and carrot and cook gently until soft. Add the fennel seeds, chile, and garlic and stir, then add the tomatoes, chopping them as they cook. Season and simmer for 15 minutes, stirring occasionally. Add the beans and stock, and cook for 15 minutes longer.

Discard the stems from the cavolo and boil the leaves in salted water for 5 minutes. Drain and chop, reserving 4 tbsp of the water. Add the water and cavolo to the soup. Stir and season.

Cut the bread into 1/2-inch slices. Grill on both sides, then rub with the remaining garlic and drizzle with olive oil. Break up the toast and divide between the soup bowls. Spoon over the soup and serve with more olive oil.

All bean soups are made more delicious with a generous addition of spicy-flavored, newly pressed olive oil poured over each serving. Tuscan olive oil is pressed at the end of October, when the frosty weather starts and *cavolo nero* (black Tuscan cabbage) is ready to be picked.

# 4

# Pea, pancetta, and zucchini

| | |
|---|---|
| Podded peas | 3 cups |
| Pancetta slices | 4 |
| Zucchini | 2 lbs |
| Garlic cloves | 2 |
| Red onion | 1 |
| Mint leaves | 3 tbsp |
| Chicken stock | 1 cup |
| Heavy cream | 2/3 cup |
| Ex.v.olive oil | |

Cut the zucchini into small pieces. Peel and chop the garlic and onion, and cut the pancetta into matchsticks. Chop the mint.

In a thick-bottomed pan heat 2 tbsp olive oil and gently fry the onion with the pancetta. Cook until soft, then add the garlic and zucchini. Stir and cook for 15 minutes. Add 2 tbsp water to loosen.

Boil the peas in salted water, drain, and add to the zucchini. Add the stock and bring to a boil. Cook for 5 minutes longer.

Pulse-chop in a food processor. Return to the pan, add the chopped mint and cream and stir. Season and serve at room temperature.

# 5            Artichoke and potato

| | |
|---|---:|
| Artichokes | 6 small |
| Potatoes | 1/2 lb |
| Garlic cloves | 3 |
| Dried chile | 1 |
| Parsley leaves | 4 tbsp |
| Chicken stock | 2 1/4 cups |
| Ciabatta loaf | 1 |
| Ex.v.olive oil | |

To prepare the artichokes, break off the outer leaves until you get to the tender heart. Cut off the tips and peel the stems. Cut into eighths and remove any choke.

Peel the potatoes and cut into pieces the same size as the artichokes. Peel and chop the garlic. Crumble the chile and chop the parsley.

Heat 3 tbsp olive oil in a thick-bottomed pan. Lightly brown the artichokes, add the garlic, dried chile, and 1 tbsp of the parsley. Add half the stock and 1 cup of water, season and cover. Simmer for 15 minutes.

Add the potatoes and the rest of the stock: there should be just enough to cover the soup. Cook until the potatoes are soft.

Cut ciabatta into 1/2-inch slices, toast on both sides, rub with garlic, and drizzle with olive oil.

Mash the soup – which should be thick – to a rough consistency. Stir in the remaining parsley and pour over olive oil. Serve with a crostini.

Preparing artichokes is easier if you use a "Y"-shaped potato peeler for trimming the hearts and stems and a melon baller for removing the chokes.

# 6 Rice and potato

| | |
|---|---|
| Risotto rice | 1 cup |
| Potatoes | 1 lb |
| Red onion | 1 |
| Carrots | 2 |
| Celery stalks | 2 |
| Parsley leaves | 3 tbsp |
| Pecorino | 3 oz |
| Ex.v.olive oil | 3 tbsp |
| Chicken stock | 2 cups |
| Bay leaves | 2 |

Peel the potatoes and cut into $1/4$-inch cubes. Peel and finely chop the onion, carrots, and celery. Chop the parsley and grate the pecorino.

In a thick-bottomed pan, heat the olive oil, add the onion, carrot, and celery, and cook until soft. Add the potato and cook for 5 minutes until lightly colored. Stir in half the stock and the bay. Stir and scrape up the vegetables and simmer for 20 minutes.

Add the rice and the remaining stock, season and cook, stirring, for 20 minutes longer until the rice is tender. Add more stock if the soup is too thick.

Stir the parsley into the soup and serve with pecorino.

This soup has very subtle flavors, so it is worth the effort of making your own chicken stock.

# 7

# Clam and fennel

| | |
|---|---|
| Clams | 3 lbs |
| Fennel bulbs | 2 |
| Parsley leaves | 3 tbsp |
| Dried chiles | 2 |
| Garlic cloves | 4 |
| White wine | 1 cup |
| Ciabatta loaf | 1 |
| Lemon | 1 |
| Ex.v.olive oil | |

Clean the clams. Finely slice the fennel, keeping the leafy tops, chop the parsley, crumble the chiles, and peel and finely chop 3 of the garlic cloves.

Boil the fennel in salted water until tender. Drain.

Heat 2 tbsp olive oil in a thick-bottomed pan, add the garlic and chile, and cook until soft. Add the clams, fennel, and wine. Cover and cook until the clams open – a few minutes. Discard any that remain closed. Add the parsley and the fennel tops and season.

Cut the bread into 3/4-inch slices. Toast, rub with the remaining garlic clove, and put into warm bowls. Pour the clams, fennel, and juices over. Drizzle with olive oil and serve with lemon.

# 8

# Zucchini and cannellini

| | |
|---|---|
| Zucchini | 1½ lbs |
| Can cannellini beans | 14 oz |
| Celery head | 1 |
| Garlic clove | 1 |
| Parsley leaves | 3 tbsp |
| Ex.v.olive oil | |

Finely chop the pale celery heart. Cut the zucchini into halves lengthwise and roughly cut them to make small pieces. Peel and finely chop the garlic and chop the parsley. Drain and rinse the beans.

Heat 1 tbsp olive oil in a thick-bottomed pan and fry the celery and parsley until soft. Add the garlic and zucchini and fry for 10 minutes. Add 5 tbsp water and scrape up to combine. Add the beans. Stir and cook for 5 minutes longer. Mash roughly and drizzle with olive oil.

Fresh cannellini beans sold in their pods are absolutely delicious and can be found in specialist stores throughout July and August. Dried cannellini beans are good too, but you have to plan ahead, as the beans need to be soaked for at least 12 hours before cooking (see page 261). Canned cannellini beans, rinsed thoroughly, can also be used for this recipe.

# 9

# Pumpkin crostini

| | |
|---|---|
| Pumpkin | 1 1/2 lbs |
| Pancetta | 4 oz |
| Garlic cloves | 2 |
| Red onions | 2 |
| Fennel bulb | 1 |
| Parsley | 2 oz |
| Dried chile | 1 |
| Fennel seeds | 1 tbsp |
| Can tomatoes | 14 oz |
| Sourdough loaf | 1/4 |
| Ex.v.olive oil | |

Peel and cut the pumpkin into 3/4-inch cubes. Cut the pancetta into matchsticks. Peel and chop 1 garlic clove, the onions, and the parsley and slice and chop the fennel. Crumble the chile and grind the fennel seeds.

In a thick-bottomed pan, heat 2 tbsp olive oil and gently fry the pancetta, then add the onion, fennel, garlic, chile, and fennel seeds. Season and cook for 5 minutes. Add the pumpkin and stir to combine. Add the tomatoes, breaking them up, and season. Cover and simmer for 15 minutes or until the vegetables are soft.

Cut the bread into 1/2-inch slices. Grill on both sides, rub with the remaining peeled garlic clove and put in the bowls. Spoon the soup over and drizzle with olive oil.

Butternut squash, with its bright orange flesh and slightly dry, potatolike texture, is an excellent pumpkin substitution for this soup.

# 10

# Quick fish

| | |
|---|---:|
| Crayfish | 4-8 |
| Clams | 1 lb |
| Ocean perch | 12 oz |
| Potatoes | 12 oz |
| Garlic cloves | 2 |
| Dried chiles | 2 |
| Parsley leaves | 2 tbsp |
| Fresh gingerroot | 2 oz |
| Lemon | 1 |
| Can chopped tomatoes | 14 oz |
| White wine | 2/3 cup |
| Ex.v.olive oil | |

Peel the potatoes and the garlic. Quarter the potatoes, slice the garlic, crumble the chiles, and chop the parsley. Grate the ginger and squeeze the lemon.

Heat 2 tbsp olive oil in a thick-bottomed pan. Add the potatoes, garlic, and chiles and cook to color.

Add the tomatoes to the potatoes and season. Cook for 15 minutes, or until the potatoes are soft.

Stir in the ginger. Add all the fish and then pour over the lemon juice and the wine. Season and cover. Simmer for 5 minutes. The clams should be open and the crayfish firm.

Add the parsley and serve with olive oil drizzled over.

Ask the fish merchant to fillet the ocean perch, also known as rockfish.

To serve 4 people, you will need 8 small or 4 large crayfish.

# 11

# Chickpea and shrimp

| | |
|---|---|
| Can chickpeas | 14 oz |
| Shelled shrimp | 1 lb |
| Dried porcini | 1 oz |
| Garlic cloves | 3 |
| Dried chiles | 2 |
| Dried oregano | 2 tbsp |
| Can chopped tomatoes | 14 oz |
| Lemon | 1/2 |
| Ciabatta loaf | 1 |
| Ex.v.olive oil | |

Soak the porcini in 1 cup hot water. Drain and rinse the chickpeas. Peel and chop 2 garlic cloves, and crumble the chiles.

Strain the porcini, keeping the liquid, and roughly chop.

Heat a thick-bottomed pan with 2 tbsp olive oil, add half the chopped garlic, the porcini, oregano, and chile and season. Cook for 4 minutes. Add the tomatoes, and simmer for 20 minutes, adding a little of the porcini water as the tomatoes reduce, to keep the soup liquid.

In a separate pan, heat 1 tbsp olive oil and add the remaining chopped garlic. When colored, add the shrimp and chickpeas and stir to warm through. Season. Add the juice of the 1/2 lemon. Mix together with the tomato.

Cut the bread into slices. Grill on both sides, rub with remaining peeled garlic clove and put in bowls. Pour the soup over and drizzle with olive oil.

**1** Sardinian bottarga

**2** Butter and cheese

**3** Marinated raw tomato

**4** Garlic, chile, and parsley

**5** Pea and scallion

**6** Tomato and anchovy

**7** Clam and Prosecco

**8** Zucchini and caper

**9** Spaghetti in a bag

# Spaghetti

# 1

# Sardinian bottarga

| | |
|---|---|
| Spaghetti | 16 oz |
| Bottarga | 8 oz |
| Lemons | 3 |
| Dried chiles | 2 |
| Ex.v.olive oil | 7 tbsp |

Squeeze the juice of 2 of the lemons. Crumble the chiles.

Grate 3/4 of the bottarga into a bowl. Add the lemon juice and stir to combine to a cream. Slowly add the olive oil to form a thick sauce.

Cook the spaghetti in boiling salted water until al dente. Drain and reserve a little of the cooking water.

Stir the hot water into the bottarga cream to loosen, then season with chiles and black pepper. Add the spaghetti to the sauce and toss to coat thoroughly.

Serve with the remaining bottarga grated over and a piece of lemon.

In this recipe, use *bottarga di mugine*, which is the sun-dried, salted roe of the gray mullet (see suppliers' list, page 263).

o.uk

a to salted boiling water and
70-80ml of olive oil. Drain
e in serving bowl with finely
Bottarga per person.

# 2

# Butter and cheese

| | |
|---|---|
| Spaghetti | 16 oz |
| Unsalted butter | 7 tbsp |
| Pecorino Romano | 2 oz |
| Parmesan | 2 oz |

Cook the spaghetti in boiling salted water until al dente. Grate the cheeses while the pasta is cooking. Drain, reserving 4 tbsp of the water.

Put the reserved water and the butter back into the hot pan and simmer very gently over low heat. Stir until the butter melts into the water. Remove from the heat and stir in half the pecorino and Parmesan. Add the spaghetti and toss to coat thoroughly. Serve with more Parmesan and pecorino.

This simple combination of pecorino and Parmesan is found in many Roman trattorias where it is called *cacio e pepe*. Made with sheep milk, pecorino from different regions in Italy varies greatly in flavor and texture. Pecorino Romano, used mostly in cooking, is a hard, strongly flavored aged cheese found in the south of Italy.

# 3

## Marinated raw tomato

| | |
|---|---|
| Spaghetti | 16 oz |
| Cherry tomatoes | 1¼ lbs |
| Basil leaves | 3 tbsp |
| Red wine vinegar | 2 tbsp |
| Balsamic vinegar | 1 tbsp |
| Ex.v.olive oil | |

Cut the tomatoes in half and squeeze to remove juice and seeds. Tear the basil.

In a bowl, combine 6 tbsp olive oil with the vinegars and season. Add the tomato halves, slightly pressing the tomatoes down to absorb the flavor of the vinegar and olive oil. Add the basil, stir, cover, and leave to marinate for an hour. Do not refrigerate.

Cook the spaghetti in boiling salted water until al dente. Drain and return to the pan. Add the tomatoes over high heat. Stir to combine. Drizzle with olive oil.

# 4

## Garlic, chiles, and parsley

| | |
|---|---|
| Spaghetti | 16 oz |
| Garlic cloves | 6 |
| Dried chiles | 3 |
| Parsley leaves | 10 tbsp |
| Ex.v.olive oil | ½ cup |
| Lemon | ½ |

Peel and cut the garlic into slices. Chop the parsley and crumble the chiles. In a thick-bottomed pan, heat the olive oil and gently fry the garlic until soft but not brown. Add the chiles and squeeze over lemon juice. Remove from heat, then stir in the parsley. Season.

Cook the spaghetti in boiling salted water until al dente. Drain and stir in the garlic sauce. Drizzle with olive oil.

# 5

# Pea and scallion

| | |
|---|---|
| Spaghetti | 16 oz |
| Podded peas | 2$\frac{1}{2}$ cups |
| Scallions | 4 oz |
| Garlic clove | 1 |
| Prosciutto | 4 oz |
| Parsley leaves | 2 tbsp |
| Parmesan | 2 oz |
| Unsalted butter | 7 tbsp |
| Ex.v.olive oil | |

Roughly chop the white part of the scallions. Peel and finely chop the garlic and tear the prosciutto into pieces. Chop the parsley. Grate the Parmesan.

Melt the butter in a large skillet. Add the scallions and gently soften, then add the peas, salt, and 3 tbsp of hot water. Simmer gently until the water evaporates.

Add the garlic and parsley to the peas plus 3 tbsp olive oil. Cover and cook over low heat for 15 minutes. Add the prosciutto. If more liquid is needed, add olive oil, not water. When the peas are soft and a dark green color, remove from heat.

Cook the spaghetti in boiling salted water until al dente, then drain. Add to the peas and serve with Parmesan.

**6**

# Tomato and anchovy

| | |
|---|---|
| Spaghetti | 16 oz |
| Cherry tomatoes | 1 1/2 lbs |
| Anchovy fillets | 10 |
| Lemon | 1 |
| Garlic cloves | 2 |
| Dried chiles | 2 |
| Basil leaves | 3 tbsp |
| Ex.v.olive oil | |

Cut the tomatoes in half and squeeze out seeds and juice. Squeeze the lemon.

Peel and finely chop the garlic, crumble the chiles, and rinse the anchovies. Tear the basil leaves.

Heat 3 tbsp olive oil in a thick-bottomed pan, add the garlic and chiles, and fry for a minute, then add the anchovies and 3 tbsp of water. Add the tomatoes and lemon juice and season. Raise the heat, cook for 2-3 minutes, stirring to combine. Remove from the heat and add the basil.

Cook the spaghetti in boiling salted water until al dente, drain and add to the sauce. Toss to coat the spaghetti thoroughly. Serve with olive oil drizzled over.

# 7

## Clam and Prosecco

| | |
|---|---:|
| Spaghetti | 16 oz |
| Small clams | 7 lbs |
| Prosecco | 1 cup |
| Garlic cloves | 3 |
| Parsley leaves | 2 tbsp |
| Dried chiles | 2 |
| Ex.v.olive oil | 3 tbsp |
| Lemons | 2 |

Wash the clams. Peel and finely chop the garlic, chop the parsley, and crumble the chile.

Heat the olive oil in a thick-bottomed pan. Add the garlic and cook until just colored. Add the chiles, the clams and Prosecco, cover and cook over high heat to open the clams – about 3 minutes. Discard any clams that do not open. Season and keep warm.

Cook the spaghetti in boiling salted water until al dente, drain, and add to the clam sauce. Cook together over high heat for 2 minutes, tossing thoroughly. Remove any empty shells. Serve with the parsley and lemon.

# 8

# Zucchini and caper

| | |
|---|---|
| Spaghetti | 16 oz |
| Zucchini | 1 lb |
| Garlic cloves | 2 |
| Dried chiles | 2 |
| Capers | 3 tbsp |
| Sea salt | 1 tbsp |
| Tomatoes | 9 oz |
| Dried oregano | 2 tsp |
| White wine vinegar | 2 tbsp |
| Oregano leaves | 2 tsp |
| Ex.v.olive oil | |

Cut the zucchini (see note below), peel and chop the garlic, and crumble the chiles. Rinse the capers. Place the zucchini in a colander, scatter with the sea salt, and leave for 15 minutes. Squeeze and pat dry.

Cut the tomatoes in half, or quarters if large. Squeeze out the juice and seeds, reserving the juice. Combine the tomato pieces with the juice, then add the capers, chiles, dried oregano, and garlic. Stir in 3 tbsp olive oil and the vinegar and season. Leave to marinate for 15 minutes.

Heat 2 tbsp olive oil in a thick-bottomed skillet. When hot, add the zucchini and fry to lightly brown. Season. Stir in the tomatoes and remove from the heat.

Cook the spaghetti in boiling salted water until al dente, then drain. Add to the sauce, turn to coat each strand, then mix in the fresh oregano and drizzle with olive oil.

If your zucchini are large, 5 inches or bigger, try this method for cutting them into matchsticks: slice the zucchini into 1/4-inch disks, then cut each disk into 1/4-inch-wide strips.

**9**

# Spaghetti in a bag

Spaghetti                  16 oz
Tomato sauce               4 tbsp
Garlic cloves                   2
Fresh red chile                 1
Shelled shrimp            1¹/2 lbs
Basil leaves               2 tbsp
White wine                ¹/2 cup
Lemons                          2
Ex.v.olive oil

Heat the oven to 400°F. Make the Quick Tomato sauce (see page 259).

Cook the spaghetti in boiling salted water for only 7 minutes, then drain. Put in a bowl and season, add 3 tbsp olive oil and toss.

Peel and finely chop the garlic, and seed and finely chop the chile.

Heat 1 tbsp olive oil in a thick-bottomed pan, add the garlic and, when colored, add the shrimp and chile, and season. Cook to heat through.

To make the bags, cut foil into 4 x 20-inch pieces. Drizzle with olive oil. Divide the spaghetti into 4 portions, and place in the center of each piece of foil. Spoon over 1 tbsp hot tomato sauce, a quarter of the shrimp, and a few basil leaves. Bring the edges of the foil together and fold to seal, leaving the top open. Pour 2 tbsp wine into each bag, then seal the top.

Place the bags in a roasting pan in the oven and bake for 6-8 minutes until they inflate. Serve in the bags with lemon.

**1**

Penne
arrabbiata

**2**

Penne, mussels,
zucchini

**3**

Penne, sausage,
ricotta

**4**

Penne, zucchini,
butter

**5**

Rigatoni,
cabbage, fontina

**6**

Orecchiette,
broccoli

**7**

Spirale, clams,
shrimp

**8**

Fusilli
carbonara

# Short pasta

# 1

# Penne arrabbiata

| | |
|---|---|
| Penne | 16 oz |
| Garlic cloves | 2 |
| Plum tomatoes | 1½ lbs |
| Ex.v.olive oil | 2 tbsp |
| Dried chiles | 4 |
| Basil leaves | 3 tbsp |

Peel the garlic and cut in half. Peel the tomatoes (see page 260) and roughly chop.

Heat the olive oil in a thick-bottomed pan and add the garlic and whole chiles. When the garlic is brown, remove with the chiles and save. Put the basil in the hot oil for a few moments to flavor it, then remove. Add the tomatoes to the olive oil and season. Cook gently for 10 minutes.

Cook the penne in boiling salted water until al dente. Drain.

Add the garlic, chiles, and basil to the pasta. Stir in the tomato sauce, mixing well.

This easy arrabbiata sauce relies on flavoring the olive oil with the whole garlic pieces, whole chiles, and the basil leaves before adding the tomatoes.

# 2

# Penne, mussels, zucchini

| | |
|---|---|
| Penne | 16 oz |
| Mussels | 2¼ lbs |
| Zucchini | 1½ lbs |
| Garlic cloves | 2 |
| Dried chiles | 2 |
| Basil leaves | 3 tbsp |
| Parmesan | 2 oz |
| Ex.v.olive oil | |

Scrub the mussels. Discard any that do not close when tapped on the side of the sink.

Cut the zucchini at an angle into ½-inch disks. Cut each disk into 3 sticks. Scatter with salt and leave to drain for 10 minutes. Pat dry. Peel and chop the garlic and crumble the chiles. Grate the Parmesan.

Heat 3 tbsp olive oil in a thick-bottomed pan, add the zucchini, and fry until brown. Add the garlic, mussels, and chiles and season. Stir and cover. Cook for 4 minutes, shaking the pan, until the mussels have opened. Add the basil. Remove half the mussels from the shells, discarding any shells that have not opened.

Cook the penne in boiling salted water until al dente, drain, and add to the sauce. Stir and serve with Parmesan.

It is unusual to put Parmesan on a seafood pasta, but this Neapolitan recipe is an exception.

# 3

# Penne, sausage, ricotta

| | |
|---|---|
| Penne | 16 oz |
| Italian link sausages | 4 |
| Ricotta | 7 tbsp |
| Tomato sauce | 6 tbsp |
| Garlic cloves | 2 |
| Onion | 1 |
| Fennel bulb | 1 |
| Ex.v.olive oil | 1 tbsp |
| Dry red wine | 2/3 cup |
| Basil leaves | 3 tbsp |
| Parmesan | 2 oz |

Make the Quick Tomato sauce (see page 259). Peel and finely chop the garlic and onion, chop the fennel, and grate the Parmesan.

Put the sausages in a skillet and cover with water. Bring to a boil, then simmer until the water evaporates. Cool, remove the meat from the casings, and crumble with your fingers.

Fry the onion and fennel in the olive oil until soft. Add the meat, wine, and the tomato sauce and cook for 10 minutes. Add the basil and season.

Cook the penne in boiling salted water until al dente, then drain. Stir in the sauce.

Place 1 tbsp ricotta on each plate. Spoon the pasta over the ricotta, but do not combine. Serve with Parmesan.

As you eat this spicy pasta, the hidden ricotta cheese comes as a delicious, soft surprise.

# Penne, zucchini, butter

| | |
|---|---|
| Penne | 16 oz |
| Zucchini | 1 1/2 lbs |
| Unsalted butter | 1 1/2 sticks |
| Garlic cloves | 2 |
| Mint leaves | 4 tbsp |
| Parmesan | 2 oz |

Trim the ends of the zucchini, cut in half lengthwise and then into approximately 1/2-inch pieces. Peel and finely chop the garlic and chop the mint. Grate the Parmesan.

Melt half the butter in a thick-bottomed pan, add the zucchini, and fry until soft. Add the garlic and season, and continue to cook, stirring, to break up the zucchini. Add the remaining butter and the mint. Smash a third of the zucchini with a fork.

Cook the penne in boiling salted water until al dente. Drain, reserving a little of the cooking water. Add it to the sauce to loosen.

Stir in the penne and serve with Parmesan.

This rich zucchini and butter sauce is a regional dish cooked in homes and trattorias from Naples to the Amalfi coast.

# 5

# Rigatoni, cabbage, fontina

| | |
|---|---|
| Rigatoni | 16 oz |
| Savoy cabbage | 1/2 |
| Fontina | 5 oz |
| Potatoes | 7 oz |
| Garlic cloves | 2 |
| Anchovy fillets | 6 |
| Dried chiles | 2 |
| Parmesan | 2 oz |
| Nutmeg | 1/2 |
| Unsalted butter | 1 stick |

Peel and slice the potatoes into 1/4-inch-thick disks. Peel and slice the garlic. Rinse the anchovies, crumble the chiles, and grate the cheeses and nutmeg.

Remove and discard the tough outer leaves of the cabbage. Cut into eighths and cook in boiling salted water until tender. Drain, then chop.

Melt half the butter in a thick-bottomed pan, add the garlic, and fry until soft. Add the anchovies and stir to "melt". Add the chiles, grated nutmeg, and the cabbage.

Cook the rigatoni in boiling salted water until al dente, adding the potatoes after 6 minutes. Drain, reserving 3 tbsp of the water. Add the pasta and potatoes to the cabbage and stir in the remaining butter. Add the fontina and a little of the pasta water. Cover for 1 minute to allow the cheese to melt into the sauce. Serve with Parmesan.

Fontina cheese melts easily and has a rich buttery taste. Use Gruyère as an alternative.

# 6 Orecchiette, broccoli

| Orecchiette | 16 oz |
| Broccoli | 1 lb |
| Pancetta | 4 oz |
| Garlic clove | 1 |
| Dried chiles | 3 |
| Parmesan | 2 oz |
| Ex.v.olive oil | 2 tbsp |

Cut the broccoli into small flowerets and the pancetta into matchsticks. Peel and finely slice the garlic and crumble the chiles. Grate the Parmesan.

Cook the broccoli in boiling salted water until soft.

In a thick-bottomed pan, heat the olive oil, add the pancetta and garlic, and cook until soft but not crisp. Add the broccoli and chiles and season. Stir over gentle heat for a few minutes.

Cook the orecchiette in boiling salted water until al dente. Drain, and add to the broccoli. Mix well, and serve with Parmesan.

It is important to cut the broccoli flowerets into pieces small enough to fit into the hollow of the orechiette.

# 7

## Spirale, clams, shrimp

| | |
|---|---|
| Spirale | 16 oz |
| Clams | 2¹/4 lbs |
| Shelled shrimp | 1 lb |
| Garlic cloves | 3 |
| Fresh red chile | 1 |
| Arugula leaves | 4 oz |
| White wine | ²/3 cup |
| Ex.v.olive oil | |

Peel and finely chop the garlic, seed and chop the chile, and roughly chop the arugula. Wash the clams.

In a large, thick-bottomed pan with a lid, heat 3 tbsp olive oil and add the garlic. Cook until soft, then add the clams and wine. Cover and cook until the clams have opened, about 2 minutes. Discard any that remain closed. Add the shrimp, arugula, and chile and cover again to wilt the arugula. Keep warm.

Cook the pasta in boiling salted water until al dente. Drain, and add to the clams. Heat together for a minute, season and drizzle with olive oil.

Fusilli can be used as an alternative to spirale. Shelled shrimp preserved in brine, or frozen, are equally good for this recipe.

# 8

# Fusilli carbonara

| | |
|---|---:|
| Fusilli | 16 oz |
| Prosciutto | 1 lb |
| Parmesan | 2 oz |
| Pecorino | 2 oz |
| Ex.v.olive oil | 1 tbsp |
| White wine | 2/3 cup |
| Egg yolks, organic | 5 |

Cut the prosciutto into $1/2$-inch strips. Finely grate the cheeses.

Heat the olive oil in a thick-bottomed pan and fry the prosciutto until soft, but not crisp. Add the wine, scraping up the bits.

In a bowl, combine the egg yolks and cheeses and season.

Cook the fusilli in boiling salted water until al dente. Drain, reserving a few tablespoons of the cooking water. Add to the prosciutto, then stir in the egg mixture, letting the heat of the pasta "cook" it. Serve with extra Parmesan.

**1** Fig and chile

**2** Borlotti bean

**3** Crème fraîche and arugula

**4** Green bean and tomato

**5** Prosciutto and radicchio

**6** Dried porcini and sage

# Tagliatelle

# 1

# Fig and chile

| Egg tagliatelle | 16 oz |
|---|---|
| Black figs | 8 |
| Dried chiles | 2 |
| Lemons | 2 |
| Parmesan | 2 oz |
| Ex.v.olive oil | 2 tbsp |
| Heavy cream | 1/2 cup |

Cut each fig into 8 pieces. Crumble the chiles. Grate the lemon peel of both lemons and squeeze the juice of one. Grate the Parmesan.

Bring a large pan of salted water to a boil and cook the tagliatelle until al dente.

While the tagliatelle is cooking, heat a skillet large enough for the figs in one layer. Add the olive oil and, when smoking, carefully place the figs in the pan, turning them immediately to caramelize. Season and add the chiles.

Drain the pasta. Stir the lemon zest and juice into the cream and mix into the tagliatelle. Add the figs and serve with the Parmesan.

Sweet ripe figs seasoned with chile give this lemony pasta an unusual spiciness.

# 2

## Borlotti bean

| | |
|---|---|
| Egg tagliatelle | 16 oz |
| Cooked borlotti beans | 4 cups |
| Red onion | 1 |
| Garlic cloves | 2 |
| Pancetta | 4 oz |
| Can tomatoes | 28 oz |
| Heavy cream | 3 tbsp |
| Basil leaves | 3 tbsp |
| Parmesan | 2 oz |
| Ex.v.olive oil | |

Rinse the beans if canned. Peel and chop the onion. Peel and chop the garlic. Cut the pancetta into 1/2-inch pieces.

Heat 2 tbsp olive oil in a thick-bottomed pan and fry the garlic and onion until soft. Add the pancetta and cook until translucent. Add the tomatoes and cook for 5 minutes, then stir in the beans and the cream. Cook for 5 minutes longer. Add the basil and 2 tbsp olive oil. Season.

Cook the tagliatelle in plenty of boiling salted water until al dente, then drain well, reserving a little of the cooking water. Add to the sauce to loosen.

Toss the tagliatelle with the beans. Drizzle with olive oil and serve with Parmesan.

# 3

# Crème fraîche and arugula

| | |
|---|---|
| Egg tagliatelle | 16 oz |
| Crème fraîche | 1 cup |
| Arugula leaves | 5 oz |
| Lemons | 2 |
| Parmesan | 5 oz |

Finely grate the lemon peel and squeeze the juice. Roughly chop the arugula. Grate the Parmesan.

Put the crème fraîche in a bowl, stir in the lemon juice and zest, and season.

Cook the tagliatelle in boiling salted water until al dente, drain and return to the pan. Pour over the sauce, add the arugula and half the Parmesan. Toss to combine.

Serve with the remaining Parmesan.

# 4

# Green bean and tomato

| | |
|---|---|
| Egg tagliatelle | 16 oz |
| Fine green beans | 1 lb |
| Plum tomatoes | 6 |
| Parmesan | 2 oz |
| Garlic clove | 1 |
| Heavy cream | 2/3 cup |
| Basil leaves | 3 tbsp |

Top and tail the green beans, cook in boiling salted water until tender, then drain.

Cut the tomatoes in half, remove the juice and seeds, and chop the flesh coarsely. Season. Grate the Parmesan.

Peel the garlic, add to the cream, and bring to a boil. Season. Remove the garlic, and add the tomato, green beans, and basil. Stir to combine.

Cook the tagliatelle in boiling salted water until al dente. Drain, and add to the tomato and beans. Serve with Parmesan.

This is a summer pasta. Always use the ripest tomatoes and the finest green beans.

# 5

# Prosciutto and radicchio

| | |
|---|---|
| Egg tagliatelle | 16 oz |
| Prosciutto slices | 6 |
| Radicchio head | 1 |
| Garlic clove | 1 |
| Rosemary leaves | 2 tbsp |
| Parmesan | 2 oz |
| Unsalted butter | 1 stick |

Cut the prosciutto and radicchio into ribbons the same width as the tagliatelle. Peel and finely chop the garlic. Chop the rosemary (see note below). Grate the Parmesan.

Melt half the butter in a thick-bottomed pan. Add the garlic and rosemary and cook for a minute. Add half the radicchio and prosciutto. Cook just to wilt. Remove from the heat.

Cook the tagliatelle in boiling salted water until al dente, then drain. Add the rest of the butter and half the Parmesan. Put into the cooked radicchio, then stir in the remaining radicchio and prosciutto. Toss thoroughly and serve with Parmesan.

The width of the tagliatelle you buy dictates the size of the ribbons of both the prosciutto and the radicchio. Don't prechop the rosemary, or it will turn black.

**6**

# Dried porcini and sage

| | |
|---|---|
| Egg tagliatelle | 16 oz |
| Dried porcini | 1$\frac{1}{2}$ oz |
| Sage leaves | 8 |
| Garlic cloves | 2 |
| Dried chile | 1 |
| Lemon | 1 |
| Parmesan | 2 oz |
| Unsalted butter | 7 tbsp |
| Heavy cream | 4 tbsp |

Soak the porcini in 1 cup of hot water for 20 minutes.

Peel and finely slice the garlic, chop the sage, and crumble the chile. Finely grate the peel from $\frac{1}{2}$ lemon and squeeze all the juice. Grate the Parmesan.

Drain the porcini, reserving the water. Rinse the porcini and chop. Strain the liquid through cheesecloth.

Melt the butter in a thick-bottomed pan, and add the garlic, sage, and chile. Color, then add the porcini. Fry until soft, then add 4 tbsp of the liquid and simmer until most of the juice has been absorbed. Add the cream, lemon zest, and juice, and reduce until the sauce is creamy and thick. Season.

Cook the tagliatelle in boiling salted water until al dente, then drain. Add to the sauce, and turn over to coat each ribbon. Serve with Parmesan.

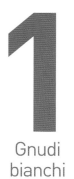 **1**
Gnudi
bianchi

 **2**
Gnudi
spinaci

 **3**
Sformata
di ricotta

 **4**
Stuffed zucchini
flowers

# Tutti ricotta

# 1

# Gnudi bianchi

| | |
|---|---|
| Soft ricotta | 2¹/₄ cups |
| Parmesan | 3¹/₂ oz |
| Nutmeg, whole | ¹/₂ |
| Semolina flour | 2 cups |
| Unsalted butter | 7 tbsp |
| Sage leaves | 3 tbsp |

These gnudi need to be made 24 hours before cooking.

Grate the Parmesan and nutmeg. Beat the ricotta with a fork, season and stir in the Parmesan and nutmeg.

Dust a flat tray generously with semolina flour. Roll the ricotta paste into short, 1-inch-thick rolls in the semolina, then cut into 1-inch pieces. Gently form the pieces into balls, coating well with the semolina, and place in the tray.

When all the gnudi are made, add more semolina in the tray so that the gnudi are slightly submerged. Leave for 24 hours in the refrigerator.

Just before serving put half the butter in a warm serving dish. Fry the sage leaves in the remaining butter.

Cook the gnudi in boiling salted water for 3 minutes, or until they rise to the surface. Transfer with a slotted spoon to the serving dish.

Serve with the sage and extra Parmesan.

"Gnudi" are just balls of soft ricotta rolled in semolina flour, which sticks to the surface to form a fine coat.

# 2 Gnudi spinaci

| | |
|---|---|
| Soft ricotta | 1 cup |
| Spinach | 9 oz |
| Parmesan | 3$\frac{1}{2}$ oz |
| Nutmeg, whole | $\frac{1}{2}$ |
| Eggs, organic | 3 |
| Semolina flour | 1 cup |
| Ex.v.olive oil | |

Cook the spinach, then drain, cool and finely chop. Grate the Parmesan and nutmeg. Separate 1 egg yolk and discard the white.

Beat the ricotta with a fork, and stir in the whole eggs one by one, then the yolk, followed by the spinach. Season, add the nutmeg, and stir in the Parmesan.

Scatter a flat tray with semolina flour, and roll and shape the gnudi as in the previous recipe. You can cook them right away.

Cook the gnudi in boiling salted water for 3 minutes, or until they rise to the surface. Transfer with a slotted spoon to a warm serving dish. Serve with extra Parmesan and a drizzle of olive oil.

Olive oil tastes the most peppery in the first three months after it has been pressed. Italian estate oils are pressed from the end of October through November, and have the production year on the label. Serve gnudi with spicy oil to contrast the sweet ricotta flavor.

# 3

# Sformata di ricotta

| | |
|---|---|
| Ricotta | 2¼ cups |
| Unsalted butter | 7 tbsp |
| Parmesan | 2 oz |
| Garlic clove | 1 |
| Cherry tomatoes | 10 oz |
| Eggs, organic | 6 |
| Crème fraîche | scant 1 cup |
| Thyme leaves | 2 tbsp |
| Ex.v.olive oil | |

Heat the oven to 400°F. Butter an oval 2-quart baking dish and grate the Parmesan. Dust the dish with Parmesan.

Peel the garlic and cut in half. Toss the tomatoes with the garlic, 1 tbsp olive oil, and season. Bake in the prepared dish for 15 minutes, then transfer to plate.

Mix the eggs and ricotta in a food processor until light. Put in a bowl and stir in the crème fraîche and half the thyme. Season.

Spoon the ricotta mixture into the baking dish, and scatter over the tomatoes and remaining thyme. Drizzle with olive oil and bake for 20 minutes.

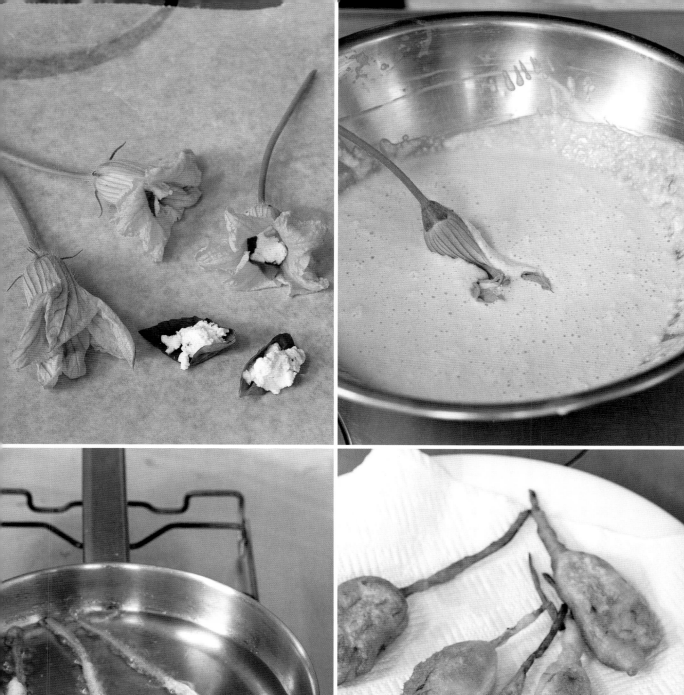

**4**

# Stuffed zucchini flowers

| | |
|---|---|
| Soft ricotta | 1 cup |
| Zucchini flowers | 20 |
| Basil leaves | 4 tbsp |
| Sunflower oil | 3 cups |
| Lemons | 2 |

Batter
| | |
|---|---|
| All-purpose flour | 1¼ cups |
| Ex.v.olive oil | 3 tbsp |
| Egg whites, organic | 3 |

For the first stage of the batter, sift the flour into a bowl, make a well in the center, pour in the olive oil, and stir to combine. Loosen this paste by slowly adding enough warm water, slightly less than 1 cup, to make a batter the consistency of heavy cream. Add 1 tsp salt, cover and leave for at least 1 hour.

To prepare the flowers, remove the stamens and the green bits at the base. Season the ricotta.

Push 1 tsp ricotta and a basil leaf inside each flower. Press together.

Heat the oil to 350°F in a deep skillet.

Beat the egg whites until stiff, then fold into the batter.

Dip the flowers one at a time into the batter. Tap gently to knock off excess, and carefully place as many as you can without touching into the hot oil. Fry until light brown, then turn to crisp the other side.

Drain on paper towels. Serve with lemon.

**1**
Fava bean
and pancetta

**2**
Fresh
tomato

**3**
Asparagus
and herb

**4**
Clam and
Pinot Grigio

**5**
Leek and
prosciutto

**6**
Porcini, sage,
and orange

**7**
Vin Santo
with prosciutto

# Risotto

# 1

# Fava bean and pancetta

| | |
|---|---|
| Risotto rice | 1¼ cups |
| Fava beans | 2¼ lbs |
| Pancetta | 2 oz |
| White onion | 1 |
| Parmesan | 3 oz |
| Chicken stock | 6 cups |
| Unsalted butter | 2 sticks |
| Extra-dry vermouth | 3 tbsp |

Peel and finely chop the onion and cut the pancetta into matchsticks. Pod the fava beans. Grate the Parmesan.

Bring the stock to a simmer and check for seasoning.

In a thick-bottomed pan, melt half the butter, then add the onion and pancetta. Cook gently to soften, then add the rice, and stir to coat each grain with the butter. Add the vermouth, stir until it is absorbed by the rice, then add the fava beans.

Add hot stock, ladle by ladle, only adding more when the last addition has been absorbed. Stir, and continue adding the stock until the rice is cooked – about 20 minutes.

Stir in the remaining butter and Parmesan.

# 2

# Fresh tomato

| | |
|---|---|
| Risotto rice | 1¼ cups |
| Tomato sauce | 4 tbsp |
| Plum tomatoes | 6 |
| Red onions | 1 |
| Garlic clove | 1 |
| Parmesan | 3 oz |
| Ex.v.olive oil | 2 tbsp |
| Basil leaves | 5 tbsp |
| Chicken stock | 6 cups |
| Unsalted butter | 2 sticks |
| Thyme leaves | 1 tbsp |
| Extradry vermouth | ½ cup |

Make the Quick Tomato sauce (see page 259). Peel and roughly chop the tomatoes (see page 260). Peel and chop the onions and the garlic. Grate the Parmesan.

Put the tomatoes in a bowl, season and add olive oil and basil.

Bring the stock to a simmer. Check seasoning.

Melt half of the butter in a thick-bottomed pan, add the onion, cook until soft, then add the thyme and garlic. Add the rice and stir to coat each grain with the butter. Add the vermouth, stirring until it is absorbed, then add the warmed tomato sauce. Season.

Add hot stock, ladle by ladle, only adding more when the last has been absorbed. Stir and continue adding the stock until the rice is cooked, about 20 minutes.

Remove from the heat, and stir in the marinated tomatoes, then the remaining butter and Parmesan.

# 3

# Asparagus and herb

| | |
|---|---|
| Risotto rice | 1¹/₄ cups |
| Asparagus | 1³/₄ lbs |
| Parsley leaves | 1 tbsp |
| Mint leaves | 1 tbsp |
| Basil leaves | 1 tbsp |
| Red onion | 1 |
| Parmesan | 2 oz |
| Chicken stock | 6 cups |
| Unsalted butter | 7 tbsp |
| Ex.v.olive oil | 3 tbsp |
| Extra-dry vermouth | 5 tbsp |

Cut the tips off the asparagus, and roughly chop the stems.

Roughly chop the parsley, mint, and basil. Peel and finely chop the onion. Grate the Parmesan.

Bring the stock to a simmer. Check seasoning.

In a thick-bottomed pan, melt half the butter with the olive oil. Add the onion and half the herbs and cook until soft. Add the rice and stir to coat each grain. Add the vermouth and stir until absorbed. Add the asparagus and stir.

Add hot stock, ladle by ladle, only adding more when the last has been absorbed. Stir and continue adding the stock until the rice is cooked, about 20 minutes.

Remove from the heat and stir in the remaining herbs, butter and Parmesan.

# 4

# Clam and Pinot Grigio

| | |
|---|---|
| Risotto rice | 1¼ cups |
| Clams | 2¼ lbs |
| Pinot Grigio | 1½ cups |
| Garlic cloves | 4 |
| Dried chiles | 3 |
| Parsley leaves | 3 tbsp |
| Stock | 4 cups |
| Ex.v.olive oil | 3 tbsp |
| Unsalted butter | 2 tbsp |
| Mascarpone | ⅔ cup |
| Lemon | 1 |

Scrub the clams. Peel and chop the garlic, crumble the chiles and chop the parsley.

Bring the stock to a simmer. Check seasoning.

To cook the clams, heat the olive oil in a thick-bottomed pan and add half the garlic and the chiles. Add the clams and half the wine, cover and cook to open. Discard any that do not open. Season. When cool, remove the clams from their shells, keeping them moist in their juices.

Melt the butter in a thick-bottomed pan, add the remaining garlic and cook until lightly colored. Add the rice and stir to coat each grain with the butter. Add the remainder of the wine, stir, and reduce. Add the stock, ladle by ladle, only adding more when the last has been absorbed. Continue adding stock until the rice is cooked, about 20 minutes. In the last few minutes add the clams and their juices.

Remove from the heat and stir in the mascarpone and parsley. Serve with lemon.

Although this is a fish risotto, chicken or vegetable stock can be used.

# 5

## Leek and prosciutto

| | |
|---|---:|
| Risotto rice | 1¼ cups |
| Small leeks | 1½ lbs |
| Prosciutto slices | 8 |
| Garlic cloves | 2 |
| Parmesan | 2 oz |
| Chicken stock | 6 cups |
| Unsalted butter | 2 sticks |
| Pinot Nero | 1 bottle |
| Basil leaves | 3 tbsp |

Roughly chop the leeks. Shred the prosciutto. Peel and finely chop the garlic. Grate the Parmesan.

Bring the stock to a simmer; check seasoning.

Melt half the butter in a thick-bottomed pan, add the leeks and garlic and cook until the leeks are soft.

Add the rice and stir to combine. Add 2/3 cup of the wine to color and flavor the rice. Stir until reduced and then add the stock, ladle by ladle, allowing each ladle to be absorbed by the rice before adding the next, stirring all the time. After 10 minutes, add ladles of wine between ladles of stock until the rice is cooked, about 20 minutes.

Remove from the heat, and stir in the remaining butter, prosciutto, basil, and Parmesan.

# Porcini, sage and orange

| | |
|---|---|
| Risotto rice | 1¼ cups |
| Dried porcini | 2 oz |
| Oranges | 2 |
| Sage leaves | 4 tbsp |
| Garlic cloves | 2 |
| Parmesan | 2 oz |
| Unsalted butter | 2 sticks |

Soak the porcini in 4 cups hot water for 30 minutes. Transfer the porcini, and keep the liquid. Rinse the porcini in a strainer under cold water to remove any grit. Lay them on a board and roughly chop.

Grate the orange peel, squeeze the juice and combine in a bowl. Chop the sage and add to the juice. Peel and finely chop the garlic. Grate the Parmesan.

Strain the porcini soaking liquid and heat gently. Season.

Melt half the butter in a thick-bottomed pan, add the garlic and porcini and cook for 3 minutes to combine and soften. Add the rice and stir to coat each grain. Add a ladleful of the mushroom liquid, only adding more when the last has been absorbed. Continue adding until the rice is cooked, about 20 minutes.

Remove from the heat, stir in the orange juice and remaining butter, and half the grated Parmesan. Serve with the remaining Parmesan.

# 7

## Vin Santo with prosciutto

| | |
|---|---|
| Risotto rice | 1$\frac{1}{4}$ cups |
| Vin Santo | 1$\frac{1}{2}$ cups |
| Prosciutto slices | 8 |
| Red onion | 1 |
| Celery head | 1 |
| Parmesan | 4 oz |
| Chicken stock | 6 cups |
| Unsalted butter | 2 sticks |

Peel and finely chop the onion, and chop the inner white heart of the celery. Grate the Parmesan.

Bring the stock to a simmer; check for seasoning.

Melt half the butter in a thick-bottomed pan. Gently fry the onion and celery until soft and beginning to color. Add the rice and stir until each grain is coated. Add 1 cup of the Vin Santo, cook and stir until it has almost been absorbed by the rice, then start to stir in the hot stock, ladleful by ladleful, only adding more stock when the last has been absorbed. Continue adding stock until the rice is cooked, about 20 minutes.

Remove from the heat and stir in the remaining Vin Santo and butter and the Parmesan.

Serve with thin slices of prosciutto over the risotto.

**1** Roasted langoustines

**2** Poached langoustines

**3** Mussel pangrattato

**4** Crab with polenta

**5** Roasted whole squid

**6** Monkfish spiedini

**7** Grilled scallops

**8** Fried scallops

**9** Roasted monkfish

**10** Sea bass with potatoes

**11** Dover sole with capers

**12** Grilled tuna with fennel seeds

**13** Roasted sardines

**14** Red mullet with bay

**15** Sicilian fish stew

**Seafood**

# 1

# Roasted langoustines

| | |
|---|---|
| Langoustines or crayfish | 16 |
| Dried oregano | 2 tbsp |
| Dried chiles | 3-4 |
| Lemons | 2 |
| Ex.v.olive oil | |

Heat the oven to 425°F.

Cut each langoustine in half lengthwise. Sprinkle the flesh side with oregano and crumbled chiles and season. Drizzle with olive oil and squeeze over the juice of 1 lemon.

Heat a large roasting pan and place the langoustines on it, cut side up, side by side. Roast in the heated oven for 4-5 minutes.

Serve hot with lemon.

# 2 Poached langoustines

| | |
|---|---|
| Langoustines or crayfish | 16 |
| Fennel bulb | 1 |
| Celery head | 1 |
| Lemons | 2 |
| Black peppercorns | 1 tbsp |
| Bay leaves | 2 |
| White wine | 2/3 cup |

Cut the fennel into quarters and the celery in half. Squeeze one of the lemons.

Bring a large pan of water to a boil. Add the vegetables, seasonings, and wine and return to a boil. Add the langoustines, pushing them down so they are submerged. Cover and cook until the langoustines are firm, depending on the size, 3-5 minutes. Drain. Serve with Aïoli (see page 259) and the remaining lemon.

Aïoli is a perfect sauce for both langoustines and crayfish. Fresh red chile sauce is also delicious and is very easy to make (see page 258).

# 3

# Mussel pangrattato

| | |
|---|---|
| Mussels | 5 lbs |
| Garlic cloves | 2 |
| Lemons | 3 |
| Dried chile | 1 |
| Ciabatta loaf | 1/2 |
| Oregano leaves | 2 tbsp |
| Ex.v.olive oil | 4 tbsp |
| Can tomatoes | 14 oz |
| White wine | 2/3 cup |

Scrub the mussels and discard any that do not close when tapped lightly.

Peel and chop the garlic, finely grate the peel of 1 lemon, and crumble the chile.

Remove the crust from the bread and pulse-chop in a food processor to make coarse bread crumbs. Combine the bread crumbs, lemon peel, and half the oregano. Add just enough olive oil to hold together.

Heat the remaining olive oil in a thick-bottomed pan and fry the garlic and chile. Add the tomatoes and remaining oregano, and cook for 5 minutes, breaking the tomatoes up. Season.

Add the mussels, stir, then add the wine. Cover the pan and raise the heat. Cook, shaking the pan, until the mussels open, about 5 minutes. Discard any that remain closed.

Divide the mussels between bowls. Scatter over the bread crumbs, add the juices and serve with lemon.

# Crab with polenta

| Polenta | |
|---|---|
| Cornmeal | 2 cups |
| Ex.v.olive oil | 3 tbsp |
| | |
| Garlic cloves | 2 |
| Dried chiles | 2 |
| Flat-leaf parsley | 1 tbsp |
| Ex.v.olive oil | 1 tbsp |
| Crabmeat | 1 1/2 lbs |
| Lemons | 3 |

To make the polenta, put the cornmeal in a liquid measuring cup so that it can be poured in a steady stream.

Bring 7 cups of water to a boil in a thick-bottomed pan and add 1 tsp salt. Lower the heat to a simmer and slowly add the cornmeal, stirring with a whisk until completely blended. It will now start to bubble volcanically. Reduce the heat to as low as possible and cook the polenta, stirring from time to time with a wooden spoon, for about 45 minutes. Stir in 3 tbsp of olive oil and season. The polenta is cooked when it falls away from the sides of the pan and has become dense and thick.

While the polenta is cooking, crush the chiles, peel and chop the garlic, and chop the parsley.

Heat 1 tbsp olive oil in a skillet. Add the garlic and cook until soft. Stir in the chiles and crabmeat. Cook quickly to heat the crab through. Add the parsley. Season. Squeeze over the juice of 1/2 lemon.

Spoon the polenta onto warm plates and serve with the crab mixture. Drizzle over olive oil and serve with lemon.

In Venice, fish and polenta are often served together.

# 5

# Roasted whole squid

| | |
|---|---|
| Small squid | 2¼ lbs |
| Dried chiles | 3 |
| Dried oregano | 1 tbsp |
| Lemons | 2 |
| Ex.v.olive oil | |

Heat the oven to 425°F.

To prepare the squid, hold the body in one hand and gently pull away the head and tentacles, with the soft pulp inside the sac. Cut off the tentacles and squeeze out the beak. Feel inside the body and pull out the quill. Wash the tentacles and the inside and outside of the body. Keep on the fins and skin. Pat dry.

Crumble the chiles.

Heat a roasting pan and brush with olive oil. When the olive oil is very hot, put in the squid and tentacles. Scatter over the oregano and chiles and season.

Squeeze over the juice of ½ lemon and drizzle with a little olive oil. Put in the oven and roast for 5 minutes.

Serve with lemon.

Small squid, around 3-4 inches in length, are perfect for this recipe.

**6**

# Monkfish spiedini

| Monkfish | 2 lbs |
| Fennel fronds | 2 tbsp |
| Ex.v.olive oil | 3 tbsp |
| Pancetta slices | 12 |
| Lemons | 2 |

Cut the monkfish into 16 cubes 1¼ inches square.

Chop the fennel. Put the monkfish in a bowl with the fennel and season. Add the olive oil and stir. Marinate in the refrigerator for 15 minutes.

Heat the barbecue, grill pan, or broiler.

Fold the pancetta slices into thirds about the same size as the monkfish. Using wood, metal, or rosemary-stick skewers, thread on the monkfish, alternating with the pancetta: 4 pieces of fish and 3 of pancetta per skewer.

Grill the spiedini carefully, turning from time to time. This should take about 8 minutes.

Serve with lemon.

# 7

# Grilled scallops

Shelled sea scallops    16
Lemons    2
Ex.v.olive oil

Heat the barbecue, grill pan, or broiler.

Season the scallops very generously on both sides with salt and pepper. Place on the grill until lightly brown and crisp, then turn over and grill on the other side. The scallops should be tender on the inside, crisp on the surface.

Serve with lemon and a drizzle of olive oil.

Anchovy and rosemary sauce (see page 258) goes well with all kinds of broiled or grilled fish.

# Fried scallops

| | |
|---|---|
| Shelled large sea scallops | 12 |
| Anchovy fillets | 8 |
| Lemons | 2 |
| Ex.v.olive oil | |

Season the scallops on both sides. Tear the anchovy fillets in half.

Heat a thick-bottomed skillet large enough to hold the scallops in one layer. When very, very hot, carefully place the scallops in to sear on each side. This will take seconds.

Add 1 tbsp olive oil to the pan, place the anchovies among the scallops and squeeze over the juice of 1 lemon. Fry for 1 minute until the anchovies become crisp.

Serve drizzled with olive oil and with lemon.

# 9             Roasted monkfish

| | |
|---|---|
| Monkfish tail | 4½ lbs |
| Lemons | 2 |
| Rosemary sprigs | 2 |
| Anchovy fillets | 8 |
| Ex.v.olive oil | |

Heat the oven to 425°F.

Cut 1 of the lemons across into fine slices. Season and drizzle with oil.

Heat a roasting pan and drizzle with olive oil. Place the rosemary sprigs in the pan and the fish on top. Cover with lemon slices and the anchovies. Season.

Roast in the oven until cooked. To test, pierce with a pointed knife; the juices should be opaque. Large monkfish will take 20-30 minutes.

Serve with lemon.

For this recipe, buy whole monkfish tail on the bone. Ask the fish merchant to remove the tough outer skin. A tail weighing 18 oz is ideal for one person, and it will cook in less time.

# 10

# Sea bass with potatoes

| Sea bass, whole | 5 lbs |
| Waxy potatoes | 1 3/4 lbs |
| Black olives | 3 oz |
| Capers | 2 oz |
| Thyme leaves | 3 tbsp |
| Dry white wine | 2/3 cup |
| Ex.v.olive oil | |

Heat the oven to 425°F.

Peel the potatoes and boil in salted water until just cooked. Cut them lengthwise into 2-inch-thick slices. Pit the olives. Rinse the capers.

Line a shallow roasting pan with baking parchment, drizzle with olive oil, and cover with the potatoes. Place the fish on top, and scatter over olives, capers, and thyme. Push some inside the fish and season.

Put in the oven, and after 5 minutes pour over the wine and a little more oil. Bake until the fish is cooked, about 20 minutes.

Fillet the bass and divide into 4 portions. Serve with potatoes, olives, capers, and the fish juices poured over.

# 11

# Dover sole with capers

| | |
|---|---|
| Dover sole, whole | 4 |
| Capers | 2 tbsp |
| Marjoram leaves | 2 tbsp |
| Lemons | 2 |
| Ex.v.olive oil | |

Heat the oven to 425°F.

Rinse the salt from the capers.

Heat 2 shallow roasting pans, scatter them with salt and pepper, and drizzle with olive oil. Place the fish in the pans, skin-side down.

Scatter over the capers and marjoram, season and drizzle with olive oil.

Put the pans into the oven and roast the fish for 10-15 minutes, or until the flesh comes easily away from the bone when tested with a knife.

Serve with lemon.

# 12

# Grilled tuna with fennel seeds

| | |
|---|---|
| Tuna loin | 2 lbs |
| Fennel seeds | 2 tbsp |
| Dried chiles | 2 |
| Lemon | 1 |
| Ex.v.olive oil | |

Heat the barbecue, grill pan, or broiler.

Cut the tuna into 4 equal steaks. Crush the seeds and crumble the chiles.

Season each steak with the fennel, chiles, salt and pepper. Place on the grill or under the broiler. Cook for a minute or so, then turn over and grill the other side. Squeeze the juice of the lemon over the fish and drizzle with oil.

Tuna steak is best eaten rare in the center, crisp on the outside. If you are cooking on a charcoal barbecue, grill close to the coals a minute on each side. If using a grill pan, make sure it's very, very hot, and turn the steak clockwise two or three times to make crisscross sear marks before turning over to grill the other side.

# 13

## Roasted sardines

| Sardines | 24 |
| Cherry tomatoes | 18 oz |
| Black olives | 2 oz |
| Lemons | 4 |
| Ex.v.olive oil | |

Heat the oven to 400°F.

Pierce the tomatoes with a fork. Toss with olive oil, season and bake for 15 minutes.

Pit the olives and grate the peel of 2 lemons.

Use a baking dish large enough to hold the sardines in one layer, and drizzle with olive oil. Place the sardines in the dish, side by side, and season. Sprinkle over the lemon zest, olives, and tomatoes and drizzle with olive oil. Bake for 10 minutes. Serve with lemon.

# 14

# Red mullet with bay

| | |
|---|---|
| Red mullet, whole | 4 |
| Fresh bay leaves | 40 |
| Garlic cloves | 4 |
| Lemons | 2 |
| Ex.v.olive oil | |

Wash the bay leaves. Peel and slice the garlic into slivers.

Make 3 cuts into one side of each fish, and push in a bay leaf and a piece of garlic. Do the same on the other side. Place a few bay leaves inside each fish and season. Put in a dish and pour over a generous amount of olive oil. Cover and marinate for 30 minutes or longer.

Heat the oven to 425°F.

Put the mullet in a roasting pan. Cover with the remaining bay. Place foil over loosely and bake for 20 minutes, removing the foil during the last few minutes. Serve with lemon.

About 1 lb is the ideal weight of fish per person. Ask the fish merchant to leave the livers in when cleaning the fish, as they add delicious flavor. If you can't find red mullet, ocean perch or croaker make good substitutes.

# 15

# Sicilian fish stew

| | |
|---|---|
| Mussels | 18 oz |
| Red mullet fillets | 18 oz |
| John Dory fillets | 10 oz |
| Garlic cloves | 3 |
| Coriander seeds | 1 tbsp |
| Fennel seeds | 1 tbsp |
| Can crushed tomatoes | 14 oz |
| Dry white wine | 1 cup |
| Mint leaves | 2 tbsp |
| Ciabatta loaf | 1 |
| Lemons | 2 |
| Ex.v.olive oil | |

| Fish stock | |
|---|---|
| Fish bones | 9 oz |
| Bay leaves | 2 |
| Garlic cloves | 2 |
| Fresh red chiles | 2 |
| Dry white wine | 2/3 cup |

For the stock, put the fish bones in a thick-bottomed pan with the bay leaves, peeled garlic, chiles, wine, and 1 3/4 cups water, and season. Bring to a boil and skim. Simmer for 10 minutes, then strain and put aside.

For the stew, scrub the mussels. Peel and chop 2 garlic cloves, and grind the coriander and fennel seeds. Discard any mussels that don't close when tapped.

In a thick-bottomed pan, heat 2 tbsp olive oil, add the garlic and color. Add the seeds and tomatoes, and season. Cook, breaking up the tomatoes, for 10 minutes. Transfer from the heat and puree.

Return to the pan and bring to a boil. Add the stock, mussels, mullet and John Dory. Pour in the wine and season. Cover and cook until the mussels open and the fish is cooked, about 5 minutes. Discard any mussels still closed.

Chop the mint. Cut the ciabatta into slices. Grill on both sides and rub with the remaining garlic. Place in soup bowls and pour over the fish and the broth. Add the mint and a drizzle of olive oil, and serve with lemon.

Ocean perch makes a good substitute for red mullet.

1 Chicken with nutmeg

2 Chicken in milk

3 Chicken with lemon

4 Flattened chicken

5 Boiled chicken

6 Guinea fowl with fennel

7 Grouse with bruschetta

8 Spiced pigeon

9 Pheasant with potatoes

10 Roasted quail with sage

11 Grilled partridge

12 Duck with tomatoes

**Birds**

# 1

# Chicken with nutmeg

| | |
|---|---|
| Organic chicken | 4 lbs |
| Lemon | 1 |
| Nutmeg, whole | 1/2 |
| Prosciutto slices | 4 |
| White wine | 1/2 cup |
| Ex.v.olive oil | |

Heat the oven to 375°F.

Wipe the chicken clean and trim off all excess fat. Cut the lemon in half. Grate the nutmeg.

Rub the chicken all over with the lemon, squeezing the juice into the skin. Season the skin and inside the cavity with salt, pepper, and nutmeg. Tuck the prosciutto slices into the cavity.

Put the chicken in a roasting pan, breast-side down, drizzle with olive oil and roast for 1 1/2 hours, basting from time to time. Add the wine after 30 minutes. Turn the bird breast-side up for the last 20 minutes.

Serve with the juices from the pan.

This is a simple roast chicken recipe. The unusual combination of spicy nutmeg with the prosciutto stuffing gives it a festive flavor.

# 2

# Chicken in milk

| | |
|---|---|
| Organic chicken | 4 lbs |
| Garlic cloves | 6 |
| Lemon | 1 |
| Milk | 2¼ cups |
| Unsalted butter | 5 tbsp |
| Sage leaves | 8-10 |

Wipe the chicken clean and trim off all the excess fat. Peel the garlic.

Cut the lemon in half. Rub the chicken all over with lemon, squeezing the juice into the skin and cavity. Season inside and out.

Heat the milk to boiling point.

Melt the butter in a thick-bottomed pan large enough to hold the chicken, and brown the chicken on all sides. Add the garlic and sage and fry for a minute. Put the chicken on its side, and add the milk to come halfway up the chicken. Simmer with the lid at half tilt for 1 hour. Baste the uncovered side from time to time. Turn the chicken onto its other side after 30 minutes.

The milk will reduce to make a thick, curdled sauce.

This chicken is also delicious cold.

# 3

# Chicken with lemon

| | |
|---|---|
| Organic chicken | 4 lbs |
| Lemon | 1 |
| Thyme leaves | 4 tbsp |

Heat the oven to 400°F.

Wipe the chicken clean and trim off all excess fat. Rinse the lemon and thyme.

Squash the lemon, then pierce all over with a cooking fork until soft.

Season the chicken skin and the cavity. Put the lemon and the thyme inside, and close using wooden toothpicks.

Roast the chicken in a roasting pan, breast-side down, for 1$^1$/$_2$ hours. Do not use any oil or butter: the chicken will self-baste. Turn the bird breast-side up after the first hour.

Serve with the juices.

# 4

# Flattened chicken

| | |
|---|---|
| Organic chicken | 4 lbs |
| Garlic cloves | 4 |
| Thyme leaves | 3 tbsp |
| Lemons | 1 1/2 |
| Ex.v.olive oil | |

Heat the oven to 400°F.

Wipe the inside of your flattened chicken and trim off any fat. Lay the chicken out, skin-side down, on a board. Using your finger, gently prise the skin away from the meat, creating pockets.

Peel the garlic and finely chop with the thyme, adding 1 tbsp salt. Push this mixture into the pockets and scatter the remainder over the surface. Turn the chicken over and use the seasoning that has fallen off to rub into the skin side.

Drizzle a roasting pan with olive oil. Lay the chicken skin-side up. Squeeze over the juice of 1/2 lemon and drizzle with olive oil. Roast for 30-40 minutes, basting occasionally with the juices from the pan and the remaining lemon juice.

Carve by cutting across the chicken in thick slices.

This recipe is only easy if you can get your butcher to bone the chicken for you. Ask to have it boned out through the backbone, keeping the breast in one piece, removing the carcass and the leg bones.

# 5

## Boiled chicken

| | |
|---|---|
| Organic chicken | 4 lbs |
| Celery heads | 2 |
| Young carrots | 12 |
| Potatoes | 18 oz |
| Thyme sprigs | 2 |
| Bay leaves | 3-4 |
| Black peppercorns | 2 tbsp |

| Gremolata | |
|---|---|
| Garlic cloves | 2 |
| Parsley leaves | 3 tbsp |
| Lemon | 1 |

Wipe the chicken clean and trim off all excess fat. Cut the hearts of the celery into quarters. Wash and scrub the carrots. Peel and halve the potatoes.

Bring a large thick-bottomed pan of water to a boil. Add the thyme, bay leaves, peppercorns, 2 potatoes, and salt.

When the water returns to a boil, add the chicken. Lower the heat and simmer very gently for 25 minutes. Add the remaining potatoes, the celery hearts, and carrots, and continue to simmer until the vegetables are tender and the chicken is cooked, about 30-40 minutes

For the gremolata, peel and chop the garlic, chop the parsley, grate the lemon peel, and combine.

Check the seasoning of the chicken stock and add the lemon juice. Smash some of the potatoes into the stock. Carve the chicken into 8 pieces and put into large soup bowls, with the vegetables and plenty of stock. Stir in the gremolata.

**6**

# Guinea fowl with fennel

| | |
|---|---|
| Guinea fowl | 2 |
| Garlic cloves | 4 |
| Rosemary leaves | 2 tbsp |
| Red onion | 1 |
| Fennel bulbs | 3 |
| Pancetta slices | 10 |
| White wine | 1 cup |
| Ex.v.olive oil | |

Ask the butcher to cut up each guinea fowl into 8 pieces. Wipe the pieces clean and trim off any fat.

Peel and finely chop the garlic and chop the rosemary. Peel the onion, and cut the onion and fennel into eighths. Cut the pancetta into $1/2$-inch pieces.

Heat the oven to 400°F.

Mix the garlic and rosemary with salt and pepper. Put the guinea fowl into a bowl, drizzle with olive oil and add the garlic mixture. Turn each piece over to thoroughly coat.

Put the guinea fowl in one layer in a roasting pan and scatter the fennel, red onion, and pancetta over. Drizzle with olive oil and roast for 30 minutes.

Add the wine and roast for 20 minutes longer. Raise the heat to 475°F for the last few minutes to brown.

# 7

# Grouse with bruschetta

| | |
|---|---|
| Grouse | 4 |
| Thyme sprigs | 16 |
| Unsalted butter | 1³/₄ sticks |
| Ex.v.olive oil | 1 tbsp |
| Red wine | 1¹/₂ cups |
| Sourdough loaf | 1/4 |
| Garlic clove | 1 |

Heat the oven to 425°F.

Stuff each grouse with 4 sprigs of thyme and a pat of butter. Season the outside of the grouse and inside of each cavity.

Put the birds breast-side down in a roasting pan. Drizzle over the olive oil.

Pour over 1/2 cup of the red wine. Roast for 10 minutes. Turn the birds breast-side up, pour over another 1/2 cup of wine and cook for 10 minutes longer, basting with the wine juices. Finally add the remaining wine and butter and roast for 5 minutes. Remove from the oven.

Cut the bread into 4 thick slices. Grill on both sides and rub lightly with the peeled garlic.

Press the garlic side of each piece into the juices in the pan, then turn them over onto hot plates. Place the grouse on top and pour over the remaining juices.

There is nothing more delicious than this wine/grouse-flavored bruschetta, especially when served with a bitter-leaf salad, such as watercress, Belgian endive, or dandelion. Grouse cooked for 25 minutes will be medium, not rare.

# 8

# Spiced pigeon

| | |
|---|---:|
| French pigeons or | |
| domestic squab | 4 |
| Garlic cloves | 4 |
| Dried chiles | 2 |
| Coriander seeds | 1 tbsp |
| Ex.v.olive oil | 2 tbsp |
| Cinnamon stick | 1 |
| Can crushed | |
| tomatoes | 14 oz |
| Red wine | 1½ cups |
| Nutmeg, whole | ½ |

Heat the oven to 350°F.

Peel and halve the garlic cloves, crumble the chiles, and grind the coriander seeds.

Season the pigeon insides with salt, pepper, coriander, and chiles.

Heat a thick-bottomed casserole large enough to hold all 4 pigeons, add the olive oil and, when hot, brown the birds on each side. Add the garlic, cinnamon, tomatoes, and wine, then grate in the nutmeg. Season.

Bring to a boil, then put into the oven and roast uncovered until the legs pull away easily – about 45 minutes.

Roasted squash (see page 212) goes very well with pigeon or squab cooked in this way.

# 9

Pheasant with potatoes

| | |
|---|---|
| Hen pheasants | 2 |
| Potatoes | 18 oz |
| Pancetta slices | 12 |
| Garlic cloves | 4 |
| Unsalted butter | 7 tbsp |
| Sage leaves | 2 tbsp |
| Chianti Classico | 1$\frac{1}{2}$ cups |

Heat the oven to 350°F.

Wipe the pheasants clean and trim off the fat. Peel the potatoes and cut into lengthwise quarters. Cut 8 slices pancetta into $\frac{1}{2}$-inch pieces. Peel and cut the garlic in half lengthwise. Tie 2 whole pancetta slices over each bird with string to secure. Season the cavity.

Heat half the butter in a thick-bottomed casserole large enough to hold the pheasants. Brown the birds on each side. Transfer from the pan, pour out the butter and wipe the pan with paper towels.

Melt the remaining butter in the pan, and add the garlic, sage, and pancetta pieces. Cook to soften. Add the potatoes and stir to combine. Add the pheasants, pour over the wine and bring to a boil. Cover and cook in the oven for 35 minutes.

# 10

# Roasted quail with sage

| | |
|---|---|
| Organic quail | 12 |
| Sage leaves | 5 tbsp |
| Sea salt | 5 tbsp |
| Lemons | 2 |
| Ex.v.olive oil | |

Heat the oven to 400°F.

Wipe the quail dry. Roughly chop the sage with the salt. Completely smother the quail inside and out with this mixture.

Heat a roasting pan on top of the stove, brush with olive oil and brown the birds on all sides. Put in the oven and roast until the legs come easily away from the breast and the skin is crisp. The quails should be almost overcooked. This will take at least 30 minutes.

Serve with lemon.

Organic quail are usually larger than farmed, and taste 100 percent better. Allow 3 per person. Quail cooked in this way are good for a party – you can eat them with your fingers.

# 11

# Grilled partridge

Gray-legged partridge 4
Ciabatta loaf 1/2
Dried chiles 2
Lemons 2
Ex.v.olive oil 3 tbsp

Remove the crusts from the bread. Pulse the bread to fine bread crumbs in a food processor. Crumble the chiles. Halve 1 of the lemons.

With scissors, cut away the backbone of each partridge to open the bird out flat. The easy way is to cut each side of the backbone where the thin ribs join. Push the bird flat with the ball of your hand.

Season the partridges with salt, pepper, and chiles. Drizzle over olive oil, then turn the birds. Add the bread crumbs, turning the birds so that they are fully coated in the crumbs. Leave for 30 minutes.

Heat the barbecue, grill pan, or broiler.

Grill the partridge, turning frequently, and squeeze the lemon halves over from time to time.

Partridge take up to 25 minutes to cook to slightly pink.

Serve with lemon.

# 12

# Duck with tomatoes

| | |
|---|---|
| Duck | 1 |
| Cherry tomatoes | 12 oz |
| Black olives | 4 oz |
| Red wine | 1¼ cups |

Heat the oven to 425ºF.

Wipe the duck dry, pull out excess fat and prick the thick fatty bits of the skin using a skewer, particularly the area between legs and breast. Rub the skin with salt and pepper and season the insides. Pit the olives.

Put the duck on a rack in a roasting pan, breast-side up, and roast on the lowest shelf of the oven for 20 minutes. Turn the duck over and roast for 30 minutes longer.

Lower the heat to 400ºF and pour out the fat, and roast for 15 minutes longer, breast-side up. Pour out any remaining fat, add the tomatoes, olives, and wine and roast for 15 minutes longer.

Let the duck rest for about 10 minutes before carving. Spoon the tomatoes and olives over each serving.

The tomatoes and wine make a thick, tangy sauce that goes well with this crisp roast duck.

**1**
Beef steak
Fiorentina

**2**
Arista di
maiale

**3**
Leg of lamb
with garlic

**4**
Veal
chops

**5**
Pork chops
with lemon

**6**
Grilled
beef tenderloin

**7**
Cotechino
lentils

**8**
Sausage
and wine

**9**
Lamb chops
scottadito

# Veal, lamb, pork, beef

# 1

# Beef steak Fiorentina

T-bone steak          5 lbs

Heat a barbecue, broiler or large grill pan.

Season the steak generously. Place on the grill and seal on all sides. As the steak is so thick, you must turn it frequently to prevent it from burning. It will be rare in some parts and better done in others. This will take about 15 minutes.

Carve the meat, giving each person slices of both tenderloin and sirloin.

T-bone steak is a cut of beef on the bone that combines the tenderloin and the sirloin. One steak about 2$^1$/$_4$ inches thick and weighing approximately 5 lbs is perfect for 4 people.

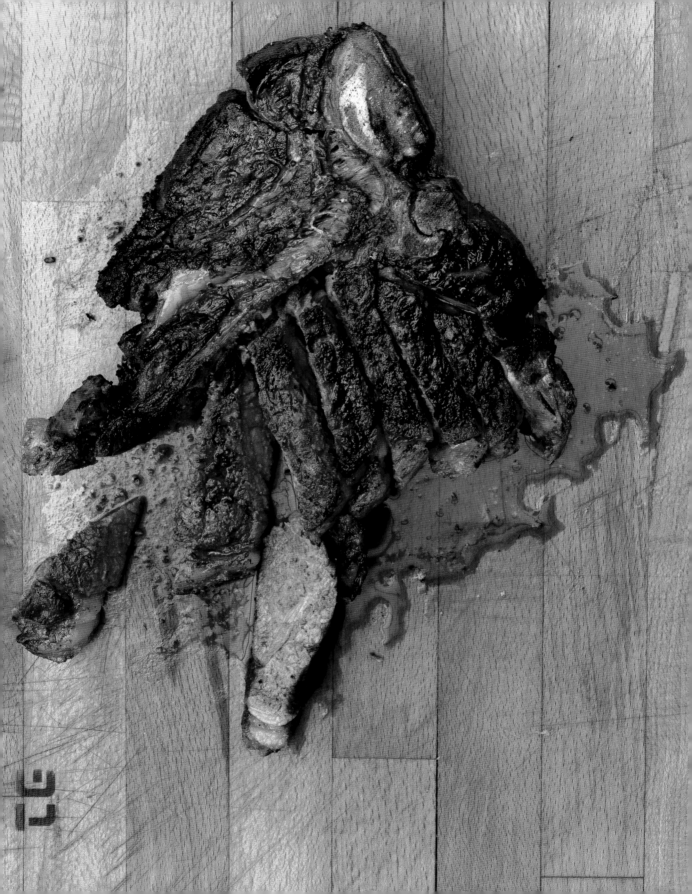

# 2

# Arista di maiale

| | |
|---|---:|
| Pork loin, boned | 3¹/₂ lbs |
| Dried chiles | 2 |
| Garlic cloves | 4 |
| Sea salt | 1 tbsp |
| Fennel seeds | 2 tbsp |
| Ex.v.olive oil | 1 tbsp |
| White wine | 1 cup |

Ask the butcher to bone out the ribs and backbone, keeping the fillet intact and leaving a little of the belly flap. Transfer the skin and some of the fat from the back. The loin will look flat, but don't have it tied up.

Heat the oven to 400°F.

Crumble the chiles. Pound the peeled garlic with salt and fennel seeds to a soft paste. Rub this into all parts of the meat. Season with black pepper and chiles. Roll the meat up, wrapping the belly flap around the fillet. Tie to secure with butcher's string every 1-1¹/₂ inches.

Heat the olive oil in a roasting pan and brown the loin on all sides. Put in the oven and roast for 20 minutes. Add the wine, baste and continue to roast for 30 minutes longer, or until the meat feels firm when pressed. Transfer from the oven and allow to rest for 5 minutes. Skim off any fat, turn the pork over and baste while resting.

Remove the string and serve cut in thick slices with the juices.

In Italy, butchers often leave the rib bones in the roll, sticking up like a rake.

# 3

## Leg of lamb with garlic

| | |
|---|---:|
| Leg of lamb | 6 lbs |
| Garlic cloves | 8 |
| Milk | 1 cup |
| Ex.v.olive oil | |

Heat the oven to 425°F.

Peel and cut the garlic cloves into slivers. With the sharp point of a knife, make slits in the fat of the lamb and insert the garlic. Rub the lamb with olive oil, salt and pepper, and put in a roasting pan. Put into the oven and roast for 15 minutes. Lower the heat to 300°F, and cook for 3 hours longer until the meat is tender and can be cut with a fork.

Remove the lamb from the pan and put on a warm plate. Skim the fat off the juices, and put the pan over medium heat. When very hot, add the milk, stirring and scraping up all the bits stuck to the pan. Lower the heat and cook until the sauce is a nutty brown color. Serve the sauce with the lamb.

# 4

# Veal chops

| Veal loin chops | 4 |
| Garlic cloves | 4 |
| Sage leaves | 4 tbsp |
| Lemon | 1 |
| Ex.v.olive oil | 2 tbsp |

Peel the garlic and chop finely. Chop the sage and grate the lemon peel. Mix together with salt and pepper.

Put the chops in a bowl, add the olive oil and squeeze in the juice of $1/2$ lemon. Add the garlic mixture, turn the chops over and marinate for 1 hour.

Heat a barbecue, broiler, or large grill pan.

Brush most of the garlic and herbs off the chops and pat dry with paper towels before grilling.

Put the chops on the grill and allow to brown lightly. Turn them over to brown on the other side. Squeeze a little lemon juice over while they cook. Turn the chops frequently so that they cook evenly. Chops $1^1/2$ inches thick will take between 10 and 15 minutes.

Chops cooked this way need to be really thick. Each should weigh about 18-20 oz.

# 5

# Pork chops with lemon

| | |
|---|---|
| Pork loin chops | 4 |
| Lemon | 1 |

Heat an ovenproof skillet or sauté pan until very hot. Heat the oven to 400°F.

Season each chop, put in the pan, and seal on each side.

Cut the lemon in half. Heat a roasting pan. Put in the chops, squeeze over the lemon juice, and place the squeezed lemon halves in the pan. Roast in the oven for 10 minutes. Press the lemon halves onto the chops and baste with the juice. Roast for another 10 minutes, or until firm to the touch.

Searing the pork chops first gives them an interesting charred flavor. Roasting the lemon with the chops and squeezing the cooked juices over the meat will result in a delicious lemony sauce to pour over at the end. Pork chops should be cut $1^1/_2$ inches thick. Serve with Salsa rossa piccante (see page 259) or Salsa verde (see page 258).

#  Grilled beef tenderloin

| | |
|---|---|
| Beef tenderloin | 4 lbs |
| Red wine | 1$^1$/$_2$ cups |
| Lemon | 1 |

Trim and season the tenderloin and put into a bowl. Pour over the wine, cover and leave to marinate for an hour, turning from time to time.

Heat a grill pan to very hot.

Cut the tenderloin across into $^1$/$_2$-inch slices. Stretch the pieces of meat out to expand, and season. Place the slices in the pan to brown on each side. This will take only 2-3 minutes.

Serve 3 or 4 slices per person with an arugula salad and lemon.

Buy the tenderloin in one whole piece and use a very sharp knife when slicing. Once marinated, the beef will keep up to 24 hours in the refrigerator. Beef cooked this way is delicious with fresh Horseradish sauce (see page 258) and Fresh borlotti bean salad (see page 38).

# 7

# Cotechino lentils

| | |
|---|---|
| Cotechino sausages | 2 |
| Lentils | 2 cups |
| Garlic clove | 1 |
| Ex.v.olive oil | 3 tbsp |
| Lemon | 1 |
| French mustard | 2 tbsp |
| Mustard fruits | |

Cook the cotechino in the foil packages, as directed on the box. Cotechino will take approximately 30 minutes to cook. Slice the cooked sausages into $1/2$-inch-thick pieces.

Put the lentils in a thick-bottomed pan with the peeled garlic, cover with water and cook for 20 minutes. Drain and return to the pan. Stir in 3 tbsp olive oil, the juice of $1/2$ lemon, the mustard, salt and pepper.

Divide the lentils between 4 warm plates and put the cotechino slices on top.

Serve with Mustard fruits (see page 230) and Salsa verde (see page 258).

Cotechino is traditionally served during the winter holiday season (see suppliers' list, page 263). Mustard fruits are a northern Italian preserve of candied fruits in a strong mustard-flavored syrup.

# 8

# Sausage and wine

| | |
|---|---|
| Italian sausages | 6 |
| Red wine | 1½ cups |
| Onion | 1 |
| Celery head | 1 |
| Carrots | 2 |
| Parsley leaves | 2 tbsp |
| Sage leaves | 2 tbsp |
| Garlic cloves | 2 |
| Cloves | 3 |
| Dried chiles | 2 |
| Can tomatoes | 14 oz |
| Ex.v.olive oil | |

Cut the sausages into ³/4-inch slices. Peel the onion. Chop the onion, celery heart, and carrot into small pieces. Chop the parsley and sage, peel and finely chop the garlic, grind the cloves, and crumble the chiles.

Heat a thick-bottomed skillet, brush with oil, add the sausage, and fry gently to release the fat and brown on each side. Transfer from the pan and pour away the fat. Add 1 tbsp olive oil to the pan, then the chopped vegetables and fry until lightly colored.

Add the garlic, sage, cloves, and chiles. Stir to combine. Add the drained tomatoes and the wine and cook for 20 minutes over medium heat until thick. Return the sausages to the pan and simmer gently for 10 minutes longer. Season.

Serve with polenta (see page 126) or Mashed potatoes with Parmesan (see page 192).

Quick-cook polenta is more convenient, but has less flavor than traditional polenta, which is easy to make, but takes 50 minutes (see page 126).

# Lamb chops scottadito

| | |
|---|---|
| Neck-end lamb chops | 16 |
| Pork lard | 2/3 cup |
| Ex.v.olive oil | 3 tbsp |
| Lemons | 2 |

Trim all the fat from the chops, and place the chops on a board. Using a flat-bladed knife, press to flatten out the meat as thin as you can, enlarging it to twice its size.

Melt the lard in the olive oil over gentle heat. Dip in each chop to coat, then place on paper towels to cool, which will solidify the lard.

Heat a large, flat skillet until very hot. Lay the chops in it side by side; you will have to do this in batches. Season and brown. This will take only 2 minutes on each side.

Serve the chops in a pile with lemon halves. Eat with your fingers while still hot.

**1**
Roast potatoes
in a pan

**2**
Potato and
fennel

**3**
Potatoes and
mustard

**4**
Stuffed
pumpkin

**5**
Potatoes
with lemon

**6**
Potato
gnocchi

**7**
Gnocchi with
prosciutto

**8**
Gnocchi with
tomato sauce

**9**
Mashed
potatoes

# Potatoes

# 1

# Roast potatoes in a pan

| Waxy potatoes | 1 1/2 lbs |
| Rosemary leaves | 2 tbsp |
| Garlic cloves | 3 |
| Ex.v.olive oil | |

Peel and cut the potatoes into 3/4-inch cubes. Chop the rosemary. Peel and cut the garlic cloves in half.

Heat a thick-bottomed pan with a lid. Add sufficient olive oil to cover the bottom. When very hot, add the potatoes, rosemary, and garlic, season generously and cover.

Cook over medium-high heat, shaking the pan to prevent the potatoes from sticking. Make sure they are turned over so they become crisp and brown on all sides. This will take 15 minutes.

This recipe is for roast potato lovers who do not have an oven in their kitchen. It is a very traditional Italian recipe and is often on the menu in Tuscan trattorias.

# 2

# Potato and fennel

| | |
|---|---|
| Waxy potatoes | 1¹/₂ lbs |
| Fennel bulbs | 1¹/₂ lbs |
| Parmesan | 4 oz |
| Garlic cloves | 6 |
| Ciabatta loaf | ¹/₂ |
| Lemon | 1 |
| Heavy cream | 1 cup |
| Unsalted butter | 7 tbsp |

Remove the outer part of the fennel and chop the leafy tops. Slice the bulbs in half lengthwise and each half into quarters. Peel the potatoes and slice lengthwise into similar-size pieces. Grate the Parmesan. Peel the garlic.

Make bread crumbs with the ciabatta (see page 260), and combine with 1 tbsp of Parmesan and the fennel tops.

Cook the fennel and potatoes in boiling salted water with the peeled garlic and lemon juice for 8 minutes. Transfer the fennel and potatoes, but leave the garlic.

Heat the oven to 400°F.

Discard all but 6 tbsp of the cooking water. Add the cream and boil until the liquid thickens. Mash in the garlic and add the remaining Parmesan.

Mix the potatoes and fennel together, and season. Pour in the sauce, mix well, and put into a buttered baking dish. Dot butter on top and bake in the oven for 30 minutes. Sprinkle the bread crumbs over, dot with more butter, and bake until brown.

# 3

# Potatoes and mustard

| | |
|---|---|
| New potatoes | 2 lbs |
| Parsley leaves | 4 tbsp |
| Capers | 2 tbsp |
| French mustard | 2 tbsp |
| Red wine vinegar | 1 tbsp |
| Ex.v.olive oil | 6 tbsp |

Scrub the potatoes and cook in salted water until tender. Drain.

Chop the parsley finely, and rinse and chop the capers.

Put the potatoes in a salad bowl and mix in half the parsley and all the capers.

In a small bowl, combine the mustard and vinegar, then slowly add the olive oil drop by drop, whisking to a thick consistency, like mayonnaise. Season and gently stir into the potatoes. Scatter over the remaining parsley. Serve warm.

4

# Stuffed pumpkin

| | |
|---|---|
| Small pumpkins | 2 |
| Potatoes | 18 oz |
| Dried chiles | 2 |
| Pancetta | 5 oz |
| Garlic cloves | 3 |
| Thyme leaves | 2 tbsp |
| Ex.v.olive oil | |

Heat the oven to 425°F.

Peel the potatoes and cut into 3/4-inch cubes. Crumble the chiles and cut the pancetta into matchsticks. Peel and finely chop the garlic.

Cut off and discard the top 1/4 of each pumpkin and scoop out the seeds. Season the insides with salt, pepper, and chiles, and put in a roasting pan lined with foil. Drizzle generously over and inside the pumpkins with olive oil and bake for about 15 minutes.

Boil the potatoes for 8 minutes. Drain, place in a bowl, and add the pancetta, thyme and garlic. Season, stir, and drizzle with a little olive oil.

Spoon into the part-baked pumpkins and return to the oven for 30-40 minutes longer. Test by sticking a fork into the side of each pumpkin. The flesh should be soft and almost falling apart.

The best small pumpkin for this recipe is the onion squash, ideally 4 inches in diameter. Alternatively, use calabaza, kabocha, or acorn squash.

# 5

# Potatoes with lemon

Waxy potatoes 18 oz
Garlic cloves 2
Lemons 2
Marjoram leaves 4 tbsp
Ex.v.olive oil

Heat the oven to 425°F.

Scrub and cut the potatoes in half lengthwise, and cut each half again lengthwise. Peel and chop the garlic.

Cut the lemons in half lengthwise, cut each half into thirds, and each third in half. Put in a bowl with the potatoes, squeezing the juice out of the lemon pieces with your hands as you mix.

Add the garlic, marjoram, salt and pepper, and enough olive oil to moisten well. Tip into a baking dish.

Roast for 30 minutes until the potatoes are cooked and brown. Halfway through, turn the pieces over.

This is a good summer recipe. Its unusual lemony flavor makes it delicious hot or cold.

# 6

# Potato gnocchi

White floury
  potatoes          2¹/4 lbs
All-purpose flour   2 cups
Unsalted butter     7 tbsp
Parmesan

Wash the potatoes and keep them whole. Cook with their skins on, in boiling salted water until soft, about 20 minutes, depending on size. While still hot, peel and immediately put through a food mill or potato ricer onto a clean surface.

Sift over the flour, season, and combine rapidly to form a smooth, soft and elastic dough.

Roll into sausage-like rolls of about 3/4 inch in diameter, and cut into pieces about 1 inch long. Press each piece against the prongs of a fork to form little ridges – these will help hold the sauce.

Cook the gnocchi in boiling salted water for 3 minutes, or until they rise to the surface. Transfer with a slotted spoon to a warm dish.

Melt the butter until just soft, and combine with the gnocchi. Season and serve with Parmesan.

# 7

## Gnocchi with prosciutto

| | |
|---|---|
| Basic gnocchi recipe | 1 |
| Swiss chard leaves | 10 oz |
| Garlic cloves | 2 |
| Ex.v.olive oil | 3 tbsp |
| Prosciutto slices | 3 |
| Parmesan | |

Blanch the chard in boiling salted water. Drain, cool, then chop roughly. Peel and chop the garlic.

Heat 2 tbsp olive oil in a thick-bottomed pan and fry the garlic until soft. Add the chard and season.

Cook the gnocchi as in the previous recipe, but omit the butter. Mix the chard with the gnocchi. Tear over small pieces of the prosciutto, drizzle with olive oil and sprinkle with Parmesan.

# 8

## Gnocchi with tomato sauce

| | |
|---|---|
| Basic gnocchi recipe | 1 |
| Red onions | 3 |
| Garlic cloves | 2 |
| Ex.v.olive oil | 2 tbsp |
| Can tomatoes | 28 oz |
| Basil leaves | 3 tbsp |
| Parmesan | |

Peel and slice the onions as thinly as possible into rounds. Peel and finely slice the garlic.

Heat the olive oil in a wide, thick-bottomed pan, then add the onion and garlic. Cook over low heat until very soft, but not brown. Add the tomatoes and stir to break them up, then season. Cook slowly over low to medium heat, stirring occasionally, for at least an hour. Remove from the heat and stir in the basil.

Cook the gnocchi as in the previous recipe, but omit the butter. Serve with the tomato sauce, sprinkled with Parmesan.

# 9 Mashed potatoes

| Potatoes | 1 1/2 lbs |
| Parmesan | 2 oz |
| Nutmeg, whole | 1/2 tsp |
| Unsalted butter | 3 tbsp |
| Milk | 6 tbsp |

Peel the potatoes and cut in half. Grate the Parmesan and nutmeg. Soften the butter.

Cook the potatoes in boiling salted water until soft. Heat the milk to boiling point.

Drain and mash the potatoes. Beat in the butter, milk, and nutmeg, then fold in the Parmesan and season.

The best potatoes to use for this recipe are a floury variety, such as russets.

**1** Zucchini fritti

**2** Whole zucchini

**3** Swiss chard

**4** Peas and prosciutto

**5** Spinach and balsamic

**6** Green beans and tomatoes

**7** Fava beans and peas

**8** Cauliflower, fennel seeds

**9** Slow-cooked fennel

**10** Grilled tomatoes

**11** Dried plum tomatoes

**12** Slow-roasted tomatoes

**13** Grated zucchini

**14** Grilled radicchio

**15** Roasted squash

**Verdura**

# 1

## Zucchini fritti

| | |
|---|---|
| Zucchini | 1 1/2 lbs |
| Sunflower oil | 1 qt |

Batter
| | |
|---|---|
| All-purpose flour | 1 cup + 2 tbsp |
| Ex.v.olive oil | 3 tbsp |
| Warm water | 3 tbsp |
| Egg whites, organic | 3 |

Cut the zucchini into 2-inch-thick ovals, then cut them into thick matchsticks. Place in a colander, sprinkle with salt, and leave for 30 minutes.

For the batter, sift the flour into a bowl, make a well in the center, pour in the olive oil, and stir to combine. Loosen this paste by slowly adding enough warm water to make a batter the consistency of heavy cream. Leave for 30 minutes. Season.

Heat the oil in a high-sided pan to 375°F.

Beat the egg whites until stiff and fold into the batter.

Pat the zucchini dry, dip them in the batter, then fry in batches in the hot oil until golden and crisp. Serve immediately.

This is a recipe where you can make good use of large zucchini.

# 2

## Whole zucchini

| Zucchini | 1½ lbs |
| Garlic cloves | 2 |
| Lemon | 1 |
| Basil leaves | 3 tbsp |
| Ex.v.olive oil | 3 tbsp |

Boil the whole zucchini in salted water until tender. Drain. Trim the ends and cut lengthwise in half. Put in a colander and leave for 30 minutes, pressing gently to remove excess water. Place in a salad bowl.

Peel and chop the garlic finely and squeeze the lemon. Tear the basil.

In a bowl, combine the garlic, lemon juice and olive oil. Season, then mix into the zucchini. Scatter over the basil.

# 3

## Swiss chard

| Swiss chard | 3 lbs |
| Lemons | 2 |
| Ex.v.olive oil | 6 tbsp |

Wash the chard, cut the stems from the chard, and chop into 3/4-inch pieces. Wash the leaves and stems, keeping them separate.

Boil the chard stems until tender in salted water. Remove with a slotted spoon and drain well.

Return the water to a boil and cook the chard leaves for 5 minutes. Drain.

Squeeze the lemons, add the olive oil, and season. Dress the stems and the leaves separately.

# 4

# Peas and prosciutto

| | |
|---|---|
| Fresh peas | 4 lbs |
| Scallions | 4 |
| Garlic cloves | 2 |
| Prosciutto slices | 5 oz |
| Unsalted butter | 7 tbsp |

Pod the peas and roughly chop the white part of the scallions. Peel and chop the garlic. Chop the prosciutto.

Melt half of the butter in a skillet, add the onions and garlic, and cook slowly to soften. Do not let them brown.

Add the peas, stir to combine, then add the remaining butter and season. When the peas are tender, after about 10 minutes, add the prosciutto, turn off the heat, cover and leave for 5 minutes. Serve warm.

Verdura

# 5

## Spinach and balsamic

Spinach                 3 lbs
Ex.v.olive oil          4 tbsp
Balsamic vinegar        2 tbsp

Remove any tough stems from the
spinach. Wash well.

Boil the spinach in salted water for
3 minutes, then drain. Press gently to
remove excess moisture.

While warm, season, then add the olive oil
and balsamic vinegar.

# 6

## Green beans and tomatoes

Ripe tomatoes           10 oz
Fine green beans        1¹/₄ lbs
Garlic cloves           2
Basil leaves            2 tbsp
Ex.v.olive oil

Peel the tomatoes (see page 260), then
halve, squeezing out juice and seeds. Cut
the stem end from the green beans. Peel
and finely slice the garlic. Tear the basil.

Heat 2 tbsp olive oil in a thick-bottomed
pan and brown the garlic. Add the
tomatoes, season, cover, and cook for
15 minutes on medium heat.

Boil the beans in salted water until soft,
about 10 minutes. Drain, then stir into the
tomato sauce. Season and drizzle with
olive oil. Add the basil.

# 7

# Fava beans and peas

| | |
|---|---|
| Fava beans | 2 lbs |
| Peas | 2 lbs |
| Scallions | 5 oz |
| Spinach | 1 lb |
| Ex.v.olive oil | 5 tbsp |

Pod the fava beans and peas, and roughly chop the white part of the scallions. Remove the tough stems from the spinach, and wash.

Heat 3 tbsp olive oil in a thick-bottomed pan, add the onion and soften. Add the peas and fava beans and enough water to just cover. Season and cook slowly until the peas and beans are soft, and the liquid has been absorbed.

Boil the spinach in salted water. Drain and roughly chop.

Add the spinach to the peas and beans and cook for 5 minutes longer to combine the flavors. Season and drizzle with olive oil.

# 8

# Cauliflower, fennel seeds

| | |
|---|---|
| Cauliflower | 1 large |
| Cherry tomatoes | 10 oz |
| Dried chiles | 2 |
| Garlic cloves | 2 |
| Ex.v.olive oil | 3 tbsp |
| Fennel seeds | 2 tsp |
| Basil leaves | 3 tbsp |

Cut the white center stem from the cauliflower and discard. Break the head into flowerets. Slice each floweret in half lengthwise. Cut the tomatoes in half and squeeze out the seeds. Crumble the chiles, and peel and finely slice the garlic.

Heat a thick-bottomed pan with a lid, add the olive oil, garlic, chiles, and fennel seeds. Cook until the garlic has slightly colored, then add the cauliflower. Stir to combine the flavors and lightly brown.

Add the tomatoes, season, cover, and cook gently for 10-15 minutes. Stir in the basil.

You could add extra spice with fresh ginger and a few crushed coriander seeds.

# 9

# Slow-cooked fennel

| | |
|---|---|
| Fennel bulbs | 8 |
| Garlic cloves | 4 |
| Dried chiles | 2 |
| Fennel seeds | 1 tsp |
| Ex.v.olive oil | |

Cut the outer leaves and stems from the fennel, then cut each in half and each half into quarters. Keep the leafy tops. Peel and cut the garlic cloves in half. Crumble the chiles. Grind the fennel seeds.

Heat a thick-bottomed pan with a lid, add the olive oil, the fennel, fennel seeds, and chiles and season. Stir over high heat until the fennel begins to color, then add the garlic. Lower the heat,cover and cook quickly for 10-15 minutes until the fennel is soft.

Check for seasoning, then stir in the leafy fennel tops and drizzle with olive oil.

In Italy, extra virgin olive oil is often added to cooked vegetables just before serving, as a seasoning.

# 10

# Grilled tomatoes

Plum tomatoes      8 oz
Ex.v.olive oil
Balsamic vinegar

Heat the barbecue or a grill pan to very hot.

Cut the tomatoes in half lengthwise. Generously scatter a plate with salt and pepper and press the cut side of each tomato into the mixture.

Put the tomato halves, seasoned side down, on the grill for 2-3 minutes until charred. Carefully turn over – they will be quite soft – and cook briefly on the skin side. Place on a serving dish, charred side up, and drizzle with olive oil and a few drops of balsamic vinegar.

This way of cooking tomatoes is only suitable for fleshy varieties, such as beefsteak or plum, that have less juice and seeds.

# 11

# Dried plum tomatoes

Plum tomatoes     12
Marjoram leaves   3 tbsp
Ex.v.olive oil

Peel the tomatoes (see page 260), keeping them whole. Heat the oven to the lowest heat.

Lightly oil a cookie sheet. Put the tomatoes side by side on the sheet, season and drizzle with olive oil. Bake in the low oven for 2-2$^1/_2$ hours, gently pressing every 30 minutes to release the juices so that the tomatoes dry up and become concentrated in flavor.

Serve at room temperature drizzled with olive oil and scattered with marjoram.

Only make this recipe with ripe, plum tomatoes when they are at their best in mid-summer. Other varieties will have too much juice and won't achieve the intense flavor.

# 12

## Slow-roasted tomatoes

| | |
|---|---|
| Cherry tomatoes | 1 1/2 lbs |
| Garlic cloves | 4 |
| Dried oregano | 2 tbsp |
| Ex.v.olive oil | 3 tbsp |

Heat the oven to 325-350°F. Prick the tomatoes with a fork. Peel and halve the garlic. Put the tomatoes, oregano, garlic, and olive oil in an ovenproof pan and season. Roast for 40 minutes. Serve at room temperature.

# 13

## Grated zucchini

| | |
|---|---|
| Zucchini | 2 lbs |
| Nutmeg, whole | 1/2 |
| Parsley leaves | 2 tbsp |
| Garlic clove | 1 |
| Ex.v.olive oil | |

Wash the zucchini, dry, then grate them on the large holes of a cheese grater. Place in a colander, spread out and sprinkle with salt. Leave for 30 minutes to release water. Wrap in a clean towel and wring out the water.

Grate the nutmeg. Finely chop the parsley. Peel and finely chop the garlic.

Heat 2 tbsp olive oil in a thick-bottomed pan, add the zucchini, nutmeg, and garlic, and season. Cover and cook on medium heat for 3 minutes. Add the parsley and stir to combine. Drizzle with olive oil.

# 14

# Grilled radicchio

| Radicchio heads | 3 |
| Lemons | 2 |
| Ex.v.olive oil | |
| Balsamic vinegar | |

Heat a broiler or grill pan.

Cut the radicchio into halves through the stems, then cut each half into 8 segments through the stems to keep the leaves attached.

Put the radicchio under the broiler briefly, just long enough to wilt. Remove and place in a serving dish.

Season generously and drizzle with lemon juice, olive oil, and balsamic vinegar.

Try serving Grilled radicchio with Grilled scallops (see page 130) – the bitter flavor contrasts with the sweetness of the scallops.

# 15

# Roasted squash

| | |
|---|---|
| Squash | 2$^1$/$_2$ lbs |
| Garlic cloves | 2 |
| Dried chile | $^1$/$_4$ tsp |
| Fennel seeds | 1 tsp |
| Dried oregano | 1 tbsp |
| Thyme leaves | 1 tsp |
| Ex.v.olive oil | |

Heat the oven to 400°F.

Peel the squash. Cut butternut squash in half lengthwise, remove the seeds, then cut each half into quarters. Cut delicate squash in half lengthwise, remove the seeds and cut each half in half. Cut onion squash in half lengthwise then cut into eighths.

Peel and chop the garlic, crumble the chile, and crush the fennel seeds.

Put the squash in a bowl with the garlic, chile, fennel, oregano, and thyme, and season. Add olive oil to coat each piece.

Put the squash in a roasting pan. Bake for 20 minutes. Turn over and bake for 10 minutes longer, or until the pieces of squash are cooked and lightly brown.

The skin of squash varies: at the beginning of the season, October, it is still soft, so keep it on when roasting. In December and January the skin should be removed, as it becomes hard. Butternut squash are flesh colored, and have a soft, juicy texture when cooked. Delicate squash are oblong, striped, and taste like potatoes. Onion squash are the small, round, bright orange squash with quite dry, deep orange flesh.

1 Wild strawberries

2 Peaches in Pinot Nero

3 Raspberries with ricotta

4 Orange ice cream

5 Fig sorbet

6 Lemon ice cream

7 Fig ice cream

8 Tartufo gelato

9 Peach and lemon sorbet

10 Blackberry sorbet

11 Strawberry granita

12 Mascarpone sorbet

13 Marsala ice cream

14 Roasted almond ice cream

15 Crème anglaise

16 Pears in mustard syrup

# Fruit & ice cream

# 1

# Wild strawberries

Wild strawberries
Lemons
Superfine sugar

Squeeze the lemon juice and stir with the sugar until dissolved. Pour over the wild strawberries and marinate for 30 minutes, gently turning the fruits over in the juice.

Serve with superfine sugar sprinkled over the top.

We have not given amounts of lemon and sugar, as it depends on how many wild strawberries you have. We usually allow a pint-sized basket per person, and $1/2$ lemon and a tablespoon of sugar per pint.

# 2

# Peaches in Pinot Nero

White peaches          6
Pinot Nero        750 ml
Lemons                 2
Superfine sugar    6 tbsp

Halve the peaches and remove the pits.
Cut the lemon peel in pieces, making
sure you remove any bitter white pith.

Cut the peaches into slices $1/4$-inch thick.
Put in a deep bowl, sprinkle with sugar,
cover with the wine, and add the lemon
peel. Cover with plastic wrap and leave to
marinate for an hour in a cool place.

Serve in wine glasses.

This is an unusual recipe for marinating peaches, as they are not peeled
and are marinated in red wine rather than white. Find a young Pinot
Noir (Pinot Nero in Italian) and choose ripe, firm peaches.

# 3

# Raspberries with ricotta

| | |
|---|---|
| Raspberries | 4 cups |
| Soft ricotta | 1 cup |
| Lemon | 1 |
| Superfine sugar | 4 tbsp |

Finely grate the lemon peel and mix with the sugar. Leave for a while to allow the flavors to combine and the sugar to be absorbed.

Scatter the raspberries on a large plate. Turn the ricotta very carefully out of the tub and then slice it as finely as possible. Place these ricotta slices carefully over the raspberries. Sprinkle with the lemon sugar.

Pasteurized cow-milk ricotta is ideal for this recipe, but fresh sheep- or goat-milk ricotta, available from specialist cheese stores, can also be used; it should be eaten within a few days of being made.

# 4

| Oranges | 8 |
| --- | --- |
| Lemon | 1 |
| Superfine sugar | 1 cup |
| Heavy cream | $2^{1}/4$ cups |
| Grand Marnier | 4 tbsp |

# Orange ice cream

Finely grate the peel of the oranges and the lemon, and put in a bowl. Add the juice of 2 oranges and leave to steep.

Squeeze the juice of the remaining oranges, combine with the sugar, and cook to reduce to a thick syrup. Cool.

Whip the cream to soft peaks. Stir in the reserved juice and peel to the syrup. Add the juice of the lemon and stir into the cream. It will immediately thicken. Add the Grand Marnier.

Freeze in a shallow container, stirring three times, every 30 minutes or so, or churn in an ice cream machine.

# 5

| Black figs | 12 very ripe |
| --- | --- |
| Lemon | 1 |
| Superfine sugar | 1 cup |
| Heavy cream | $2/3$ cup |

# Fig sorbet

Squeeze the lemon. Peel the figs, leaving some skin. Put them with the lemon juice in a food processor and chop coarsely. Put in a bowl and stir in the sugar and cream.

Freeze in a shallow container, stirring three times, every 30 minutes or so, or churn in an ice-cream machine.

# 6

## Lemon ice cream

| | |
|---|---|
| Lemons | 3 |
| Superfine sugar | 1 cup |
| Heavy cream | 2 cups |
| Salt | 1/2 tsp |

Finely grate the peel of 1 of the lemons. Squeeze the juice of all 3 and combine with the sugar. Slowly add the cream and salt, mixing carefully. It will immediately thicken.

Pour into a shallow container and freeze until solid around the outside and mushy in the middle. Stir with a fork and freeze until firm, or churn in an ice-cream machine.

# 7

## Fig ice cream

| | |
|---|---|
| Black figs | 8 |
| Dark brown sugar | 3 tbsp |
| Lemon | 1/2 |
| Crème anglaise | 1 1/4 cups |

Put the figs into a bowl and pour over boiling water just to color the skin. Remove from the water and dry. Cut off the stems and chop roughly. Add the sugar and lemon juice. Stir to mix.

Stir into the Crème anglaise (see page 227). Freeze in a shallow container, stirring three times, every 30 minutes or so, or churn in an ice-cream machine.

Bought commercial crème anglaise (custard sauce) is fine to use for this ice cream.

# 8

# Tartufo gelato

| | |
|---|---|
| Chocolate 100% | 8 oz |
| Chocolate 70% | 8 oz |
| Milk | 2¹/2 cups |
| Egg yolks, organic | 4 |
| Superfine sugar | 1/2 cup |
| Heavy cream | 5 tbsp |

Break the chocolate up into small pieces. Keep separate. Heat the milk.

In a bowl, whisk the egg yolks with the sugar until thick, then add the hot milk, whisking all the time. Put in a thick-bottomed pan and cook over low heat, stirring until the mixture thickens and coats the back of a spoon. Remove from the heat.

Melt the 100% chocolate with half the 70% chocolate in a bowl over simmering water. Remove from the heat, and slowly add the hot custard, whisking all the time. Cool.

Stir in the cream. Churn in an ice cream machine or freeze in a shallow container. About 5 minutes before it is frozen, mix in the remaining pieces of 70% chocolate, and continue churning or freezing until set.

The 100 percent cocoa solids chocolate is so bitter that it is inedible on its own, but is essential to this recipe. In Rome you will find this ice cream in the "Tre Scalini" gelateria in the Piazza Navona.

# 9

## Peach and lemon sorbet

| | |
|---|---|
| Yellow peaches | 6 |
| Lemon | 1 |
| Superfine sugar | 1 cup |

Peel, pit, and chop the peaches. Finely grate the lemon peel and squeeze the juice. Combine with the sugar and leave for 30 minutes. Freeze in a shallow container, stirring three times, every 30 minutes or so, or churn in an ice-cream machine.

# 10

## Blackberry sorbet

| | |
|---|---|
| Blackberries | 1 1/2 lbs |
| Superfine sugar | 1 3/4 cups |
| Water | 2/3 cup |
| Lemon | 1/2 |

Combine the sugar and water and cook to reduce to a thick syrup. Squeeze the lemon. Pulse the blackberries in a food processor. Add the syrup and lemon juice. Freeze in a shallow container, stirring three times, every 30 minutes or so, or churn in an ice-cream machine.

# 11

## Strawberry granita

| | |
|---|---|
| Strawberries | 1 1/2 lbs |
| Superfine sugar | 1 cup |
| Balsamic vinegar | 1 tbsp |
| Lemon | 1/2 |
| Water | 4 tbsp |

Make a sugar syrup with the water and 3/4 cup of the sugar. Cool and add the vinegar.

Squeeze the lemon. With a fork, smash the strawberries with the remaining sugar. Add the lemon juice and mix with the syrup. Freeze in a shallow container, stirring three times, every 30 minutes or so, or churn in an ice-cream machine.

It is only worth making this granita if you have a sweet and thick, aged balsamic vinegar.

# 12

## Mascarpone sorbet

| | |
|---|---|
| Mascarpone | 1½ cups |
| Lemon | 1 |
| Superfine sugar | 1 cup |
| Water | 1½ cups |

Squeeze the lemon. Make a thick sugar syrup with the sugar and water. Add the lemon juice. Put the mascarpone into a bowl and stir with a whisk to lighten. Stir in the syrup. Freeze in a shallow container, stirring three times, every 30 minutes or so, or churn in an ice-cream machine.

# 13

## Marsala ice cream

| | |
|---|---|
| Egg yolks, organic | 10 |
| Superfine sugar | 1 cup |
| Dry Marsala | 1½ cups |
| Heavy cream | 2 cups |

Beat the yolks with the sugar until light and fluffy. Add 7 tbsp of the Marsala and transfer to a bowl that will fit over a thick-bottomed pan of simmering water. The water should not touch the bowl. Stir until the mixture comes up to a boil. This will take 30 minutes. Stir in the remaining Marsala. Cool.

If using an ice-cream machine, just add the cream and churn. If not, beat the cream before folding into the mixture, then freeze in a shallow container, stirring three times, every 30 minutes or so.

Extra-dry sherry is a good alternative to Marsala.

# 14

Blanched
  almonds      1½ cups
Crème anglaise  2¼ cups
Unsalted butter    1 tbsp
Superfine sugar   2 tbsp

# Roasted almond ice cream

Heat the oven to 350°F.

Make the Crème anglaise (see below). Place the almonds on a cookie sheet and bake until lightly brown. Add the butter and sugar, mix and bake for 10 minutes longer. Cool.

Put the almonds on half a kitchen cloth, fold the other half over and bash into bits with a rolling pin. Stir the almonds into the Crème anglaise. Freeze in a shallow container, stirring three times, every 30 minutes or so, or churn in an ice-cream machine.

# 15

Heavy cream    1¾ cups
Milk              ½ cup
Eggs, organic         4
Vanilla bean         1
Superfine sugar   6 tbsp

# Crème anglaise

Separate the eggs. Scrape the seeds out of the vanilla bean. In a thick-bottomed pan, combine the milk, the vanilla seeds, and the cream. Cook until just boiling.

Beat the egg yolks and sugar until pale and thick.

Pour the warm cream/milk slowly into the egg yolks and stir. Return to the saucepan and cook over low heat, stirring constantly. When it is almost at boiling point remove from heat. If it boils, the sauce will curdle. Let cool.

# 16

# Pears in mustard syrup

| | |
|---|---|
| Bartlett pears | 4 lbs |
| Dry white wine | 750 ml |
| Superfine sugar | 2 cups |
| Mustard essence | 1 tsp |

Peel the pears. Cut each pear in half lengthwise, remove the core and cut each half into 6.

Put the pears with the wine and sugar in a bowl, pressing them down into the marinade. Cover with plastic wrap touching the surface of the wine, and leave for 10 hours in the refrigerator.

Remove the pears from the marinade. Put the marinade into a thick-bottomed pan, bring to a boil, and reduce by half to a thick syrup. Add the mustard essence and stir.

Add the pears to the hot syrup. Heat your jam jars and fill with the pears. Cover and seal. Once opened keep in a refrigerator and eat within 2 weeks.

We ate mustard fruit at a wedding in Parma and were given the recipe for pears. This recipe is also suitable for apples and quinces, just follow the same procedure. The challenge is to find the mustard essence (see suppliers' list, page 263).

# 1 Ricciarelli 2 Ciambelline 3 Amaretti

## Italian biscotti

# 1

# Ricciarelli

Blanched
  almonds          1 1/2 cups
Candied orange
  peel             5 tbsp
All-purpose flour  2 tbsp
Superfine sugar    3/4 cup
Water              3 tbsp
Egg whites, organic    2
Confectioners'
  sugar            2 tsp
Baking powder      1 1/2 tsp

Rolling out
Cornstarch         1 cup
Confectioners'
  sugar            1/2 cup
Rice paper sheets    6

Put the almonds, peel, and flour in a processor and mix to a sticky paste.

Combine the superfine sugar and water, and cook for 3-4 minutes, reducing to a syrup. Cool for 30-60 seconds.

Mix the paste with the syrup and leave covered in the refrigerator for 1 hour.

Heat the oven to 275°F.

Beat the egg whites with the confectioners' sugar until stiff. Mix with the paste to loosen, then add the baking powder.

For rolling out, scatter a surface very generously with a mixture of cornstarch and confectioners' sugar. Roll the paste, incorporating some of the mixture, into a soft, flat roll 1 1/2 inches thick. Cut into slices 1/2 inch thick.

Put the slices on cookie sheets lined with rice paper. Bake in the oven for 30 minutes. The cookies will rise and have a cracked surface and a chewy center. Cool on a wire rack. Sprinkle with confectioners' sugar before serving.

The rice paper will stick firmly to the bottom of the cookies; just tear off the paper from around them.

# 2

# Ciambelline

| | |
|---|---|
| Red wine | 1 cup |
| Ex.v.olive oil | 1 cup |
| Superfine sugar | 1 cup |
| All-purpose flour | |
| Anise seeds | 2 tsp |

Put the wine, olive oil, and sugar into a bowl. Sift in as much flour as you need to make a stiff dough.

Pound the seeds and add half to the dough. Mix to distribute them evenly and wrap the dough in plastic wrap. Rest for 30 minutes.

Heat the oven to 325°F.

Divide the dough into small pieces of golf-ball size, and roll out into little finger-thick rolls. Cut into 2$^1$/2-inch pieces. Make each piece into a loop, pinching the ends together. Scatter over the remaining seeds.

Line a cookie sheet with baking parchment and brush with olive oil. Put the cookies on it and bake for 35 minutes, or until crisp. Remove from the sheet and cool on a wire rack.

This recipe comes from the Capezzana estate outside Florence. Fennel seeds may be used instead of the anise seeds. The cookies are traditionally served with a glass of Vin Santo.

# 3

| | |
|---|---|
| Blanched almonds | 2 cups |
| Superfine sugar | 1$^1$/2 cups |
| Egg whites, organic | 5 |

## Amaretti

Heat the oven to 350°F.

Put the almonds in a mortar and add $^1$/2 cup of the sugar, little by little, pounding constantly. This step is important to extract the oil from the almonds. Don't be tempted to use a food processor – it won't work.

Beat the egg whites until stiff. Fold in the remaining sugar and add the almonds.

Cut ribbons of waxed paper 2 inches wide, and put on a cookie sheeet. Put teaspoonfuls of the batter on the paper, about $^3$/4 inch apart.

Sprinkle with sugar and bake for 20 minutes. Cool on a wire rack.

**1**

Plum and
orange

**2**

Pistachio

**3**

Pine
nut

**4**

Polenta
crumble

# Almond cakes

# 1

# Plum and orange

Plums
Ripe plums                1 lb
Orange                        1
Superfine sugar       1/4 cup
Vanilla bean                 1

Cake
Blanched
  almonds              2/3 cup
Unsalted
  butter          1 1/4 sticks
Superfine sugar      3/4 cup
Eggs, organic              2
All-purpose flour     2/3 cup
Baking powder      1 1/4 tsp

Topping
Orange                        1
Unsalted butter       2 tbsp
Muscovado sugar     2 tbsp
Slivered almonds      1/2 cup

Finely grate the peel and squeeze the juice of the orange.

Heat the oven to 350°F.

Halve and pit the plums and put in a baking dish with the sugar and the orange juice and peel. Add the split vanilla bean and bake for 20 minutes. Cool. Scrape in the vanilla seeds.

Grease a 10-inch round springform pan with extra butter and line with baking parchment.

Grind the almonds in a food processor. Soften the butter and beat with the sugar until light and fluffy. Beat in the eggs one by one. Fold in the flour, baking powder, and ground almonds.

Pour into the pan and push the plums and their juices into and over the cake. Bake in the oven for 30 minutes.

For the topping, finely grate the orange peel. Melt the butter and stir in the sugar, peel, and slivered almonds. Scatter this over the half-baked cake, lower the heat to 325°F, and bake for 1 hour longer. Cool the cake in the pan.

# 2

Unsalted
  butter         2$^1$/4 sticks
Lemon                   1
Vanilla bean         1
Blanched
  almonds       2/3 cup
Pistachios        3/4 cup
Superfine sugar  1$^1$/4 cups
Eggs, organic       4
All-purpose flour   1/2 cup

Topping
Lemon                   1
Pistachios        1/2 cup
Superfine sugar    1/4 cup

# Pistachio

Heat the oven to 300°F.

Grease a 12 x 4$^1$/2 x 2$^3$/4-inch loaf pan with 4 tsp of the butter and line with baking parchment.

Soften the remaining butter. Finely grate the lemon peel. Split the vanilla bean and scrape out the seeds. Finely grind the almonds and pistachios together.

Beat the butter and the sugar until light and fluffy. Beat in the eggs, one at a time. Add the lemon peel and vanilla seeds, then fold in the nuts and sift in the flour.

Spoon the batter into the pan and bake for 45-60 minutes. The cake is ready when a skewer comes out clean. Leave to cool in the pan, then turn out.

For the topping, grate the lemon peel and squeeze the juice. Halve the pistachios. Mix the lemon juice with the sugar, boil until reduced to a syrup, then add the peel. Stir in the pistachios and pour over the cake.

# 3

# Pine nut

| | |
|---|---|
| Unsalted butter | 2¹/₄ sticks |
| Vanilla beans | 2 |
| Lemons | 2 |
| Pine nuts | 6 tbsp |
| Superfine sugar | 1¹/₄ cups |
| Eggs, organic | 4 |
| All-purpose flour | 3/4 cup |
| Ground almonds | 1 cup |
| Salt | ¹/₄ tsp |

Heat the oven to 350°F.

Grease an 8¹/₂ x 4¹/₂ x 2¹/₂-inch loaf pan with extra butter and line with baking parchment.

Soften the butter. Scrape the seeds out of the vanilla beans. Finely grate the lemon peel. Juice 1 of the lemons. Roughly chop half the pine nuts.

Beat the butter and sugar with the vanilla seeds until light and fluffy, then stir in the eggs one at a time. Fold in the flour, ground almonds, and chopped pine nuts, and stir in the lemon peel and juice.

Mix the remaining pine nuts with the salt. Spoon the mixture into the pan, sprinkle over the salted pine nuts and bake in the oven for 1 hour. The cake is ready when a skewer comes out clean. Leave to cool in the pan.

Adding a little salt to the pine nuts for the top of the cake gives them a more interesting flavor.

**4**

# Polenta crumble

| Unsalted butter | 1 stick |
| Lemon | 1 |
| Blanched almonds | 3/4 cup |
| All-purpose flour | 1 cup |
| Polenta flour | 1 cup |
| Superfine sugar | 1 cup |
| Egg yolks, organic | 2 |

Heat the oven to 350°F. Butter and flour an 8-inch round cake pan, using extra butter and flour.

Soften the butter. Finely grate the lemon peel and grind the almonds coarsely. Put the lemon peel and almonds in a bowl with the flour, polenta, and sugar. With a fork, mix in the egg yolks, and then the butter. You should have a crumbly dough.

Press this dough into the prepared pan and bake for 30 minutes. Let it cool completely before cutting.

**1**
Dark
truffle

**2**
Walnut and
brandy

**3**
15-minute

**4**
Espresso and
hazelnut

**5**
Easy small
nemesis

# Chocolate cakes

# 1

# Dark truffle

| | |
|---|---|
| Chocolate 70% | 8 oz |
| Heavy cream | 1¹/₄ cups |
| Unsweetened cocoa powder | 2 tbsp |

Break the chocolate into pieces and melt in a bowl over simmering water.

Warm the cream, then stir into the warm chocolate. Place a 6-inch cake ring on a flat plate. Pour the mixture into the ring and leave to set for 1 hour in the refrigerator.

To remove the ring, soak a dishcloth in very hot water and wrap it around the ring for 2 minutes to slightly melt the edge of the cake, making it easy to lift off the ring.

Sift the cocoa powder over the top.

# 2

## Walnut and brandy

| Shelled walnuts | 3 cups |
| Chocolate 70% | 9 oz |
| Unsalted butter | 3 sticks |
| Eggs, organic | 4 |
| Superfine sugar | 1 cup |
| Brandy | 3 tbsp |

Using extra butter, grease a 10-inch round springform cake pan and line with baking parchment. Heat the oven to 325°F.

Chop the walnuts in a food processor until they have the consistency of fine bread crumbs. Break the chocolate into pieces and melt with the butter in a bowl over a pan of simmering water.

Separate the eggs. Beat the yolks with the sugar until pale. Slowly add the melted chocolate, then fold in the walnuts. Beat the egg whites until stiff and fold into the mixture. Pour into the pan.

Bake in the oven for 15 minutes. Reduce the heat to 300°F and bake for 1 hour longer. Cool in the pan.

When cool, unmold and pour the brandy over the cake.

# 3

# 15-minute

| | |
|---|---|
| Chocolate 70% | 1 lb |
| Unsalted butter | 2½ sticks |
| Eggs, organic | 6 |

Heat the oven to 425°F. Using extra butter, grease a 10-inch springform cake pan and line with baking parchment.

Break the chocolate into pieces and melt with the butter in a bowl over simmering water.

In a separate bowl over simmering water, beat the eggs until they start to thicken, then remove from the heat and continue beating until firm peaks form.

Fold half the eggs into the melted chocolate, then fold in the remainder. Pour the batter into the pan and cover with buttered foil.

Place in a bain-marie of very hot water. It is essential, if the cake is to cook evenly, that the water comes halfway up the side of the cake pan.

Bake for 5 minutes, remove the foil, and bake for 10 minutes longer until just set. Remove from the water and cool in the pan. Unmold when completely cool.

The butter, chocolate, and eggs should all be at room temperature. If using an electric mixer, warm the bowl and beat close to the stove, while the chocolate is melting.

# 4

# Espresso and hazelnut

Shelled
  hazelnuts      3$^1$/$_2$ cups
Instant coffee      4 tbsp
Chocolate 70%      6 oz
Unsalted
  butter      2$^1$/$_2$ sticks
Eggs, organic      6
Superfine sugar      1 cup

Heat the oven to 325°F.

Using extra butter, grease a 10-inch round springform cake pan and line with baking parchment.

Roast the hazelnuts in the oven until brown. Let cool, then rub off the skins, and grind the nuts to a fine powder.

Dissolve the instant coffee in 1 tbsp hot water.

Break the chocolate into pieces and melt with the butter and coffee in a bowl over simmering water. Cool, then fold in the hazelnuts.

Separate the eggs and beat the yolks and sugar in a mixer until pale and doubled in size. Fold in the chocolate mixture.

Beat the egg whites until stiff, and then carefully fold into the batter. Pour into the pan.

Bake in the oven for 1 hour. Cool in the pan.

# 5

## Easy small nemesis

Chocolate 70%     12 oz
Unsalted butter   2 sticks
Eggs, organic            5
Superfine sugar      1 cup

Heat the oven to 300°F.

Using extra butter, grease a 10-inch round cake pan and line with baking parchment.

Break the chocolate into pieces and melt with the butter in a bowl over simmering water. Beat the eggs and 5 tbsp of the sugar in an electric mixer until the volume quadruples.

Heat the remaining sugar with 7 tbsp water until dissolved into a light syrup. Pour the hot syrup into the melted chocolate and cool slightly.

Add the chocolate to the eggs and beat slowly until the mixture is combined. Pour into the pan.

Put a folded dish towel in the bottom of a roasting pan. Put in the cake and add enough hot water to come three-quarters of the way up the side of the cake pan.

Bake in the oven for 1 hour until set. Leave the cake to cool in the water before unmolding.

# Chocolate

All the best chocolate is made up of pure cocoa solids and sugar, sometimes with the addition of natural vanilla, and cocoa butter for extra smoothness; avoid chocolate with non-cocoa vegetable fats. The amount of cocoa solids is now written as a percentage on the label of most bars. When choosing chocolate for making cakes and ice creams, aim for a cocoa solids content between 55 and 75 percent. A high percentage of cocoa solids does not, however, always guarantee high-quality chocolate. Good brands to look for are Rococo, Valrhona, El Rey, Amedei, and Green and Black's Organic.

To melt chocolate, place in a bowl over a pan of simmering water; the water should not touch the bowl. Store chocolate in a cool, dry place at 60-65°F – never in the refrigerator.

**1** Fresh red chile

**2** Anchovy and rosemary

**3** Horseradish

**4** Salsa verde

**5** Aïoli

**6** Salsa rossa piccante

**7** Quick tomato

**8** Coarse bread crumbs

**9** Peeling tomatoes

**10** Salted anchovies

**11** Dried chickpeas

**12** Borlotti and cannellini beans

# Sauces & basics

# 1 Fresh red chile

| | |
|---|---|
| Fresh chiles | 6 |
| Ex.v.olive oil | 5 tbsp |

Cut the chiles in half lengthwise, scrape out the seeds and finely chop. Season generously and cover with olive oil.

# 2 Anchovy and rosemary

| | |
|---|---|
| Anchovy fillets | 10 |
| Lemon | 1 |
| Rosemary leaves | 2 tbsp |
| Ex.v.olive oil | 4 tbsp |

Finely chop the anchovies and put into a bowl. Squeeze the lemon juice and finely chop the rosemary.

Mix the lemon juice into the anchovies to "melt" them, then stir in the rosemary and season with black pepper. Add the olive oil and mix well.

# 3 Horseradish

| | |
|---|---|
| Fresh horseradish | $3^1/_2$ oz |
| White wine vinegar | 1 tbsp |
| Lemon | $^1/_2$ |
| Crème fraîche | 1 cup |

Peel and grate the horseradish on the fine part of a cheese grater. Add the vinegar and lemon juice, season and stir in the crème fraîche.

# 4 Salsa verde

| | |
|---|---|
| Parsley leaves | 2 tbsp |
| Mint leaves | 1 tbsp |
| Basil leaves | 1 tbsp |
| Garlic clove | 1 |
| Capers | 1 tbsp |
| Anchovy fillets | 3 |
| Dijon mustard | 1 tsp |
| Red wine vinegar | 1 tbsp |
| Ex.v.olive oil | |

Finely chop the parsley, mint, and basil, put into a bowl and cover with olive oil. Peel the garlic and chop with the capers and anchovy. Add to the herbs and mix together. Stir in the mustard and vinegar, season with black pepper, and add more olive oil to loosen the sauce.

## 5 Aïoli

| Ciabatta loaf | $^1/_4$ |
| Garlic cloves | 3 |
| Egg yolk, organic | 1 |
| Ex.v.olive oil | $^3/_4$ cup |
| Lemon | $^1/_2$ |

Remove the crust from the bread and wet the bread with water. Squeeze out most of the water. Using a mortar and pestle, pound the bread with the peeled garlic and 1 tsp salt to a smooth paste. Mix in the egg yolk and then the olive oil, drop by drop, until you have a thick sauce. Squeeze in the lemon juice and season with black pepper.

## 6 Salsa rossa piccante

| Bread crumbs | 3 tbsp |
| Tomatoes | 3 |
| Fresh chiles | 4 |
| Dried oregano | 1 tbsp |
| Red wine vinegar | 1 tbsp |
| Ex.v.olive oil | |

Prepare the bread crumbs (see page 260).

Peel the tomatoes (see page 260). Cut in half, squeeze out the seeds, and chop to a pulp. Cut the chiles in half lengthwise, scrape out the seeds, and finely chop. Mix the tomato pulp with the chile then stir in the oregano. Add the bread crumbs and season. Mix in the vinegar and then add enough olive oil to make a thick sauce.

## 7 Quick tomato

| Garlic cloves | 3 |
| Basil leaves | 1 tbsp |
| Ex.v.olive oil | 2 tbsp |
| Can tomatoes | 28 oz |

Peel and slice the garlic. Heat the olive oil in a thick-bottomed pan and fry the garlic until brown. Add the tomatoes and season. Cook over a high heat, stirring for 15 minutes to break up the tomatoes as they cook preventing them from sticking. Add the basil and some extra olive oil and season.

**8**  Coarse bread crumbs

Ciabatta or sourdough loaf

Cut the crusts from the stale bread and discard. Tear the bread into small pieces and pulse-chop in the food processor.

If your bread is fresh, place in a 400°F oven for 10 minutes until it is crisp but not brown. Let cool, then pulse-chop in the food processor.

**9**  Peeling tomatoes

Use a small sharp knife and make a cut from the stem down the side of each tomato. Put in a bowl and cover with boiling water. After $1/2$ minute transfer with a slotted spoon into a bowl of cold water. Peel as soon as they are cool enough to touch.

**10**  Salted anchovies

Rinse each anchovy under slow-running cold water to remove any salt crusted to the skin, then carefully pull each fillet off the bone. Discard the head and pull off the fins and tail. Pat dry and use immediately. If using later, squeeze a little lemon juice over and cover with olive oil. They will keep like this for 2 or 3 days.

## 11  Dried chickpeas

| | |
|---|---:|
| Chickpeas | 1¼ cups |
| Baking soda | 2 tsp |
| All-purpose flour | 2 tbsp |
| Garlic cloves | 2 |
| Fresh chiles | 2 |
| Celery stalks | 2 |
| Ex.v.olive oil | |

Soak the chickpeas overnight in cold water with 1 tsp baking soda and 1 tbsp all-purpose flour.

Peel the garlic. Drain the chickpeas, rinse well and put in a pan with the remaining baking soda and flour. Cover with cold water. Add the garlic, chiles, and celery and stir.

Bring to a boil and skim off the foam that rises to the surface. Turn the heat down and simmer. After 30 minutes add 3 tbsp olive oil and 1 tsp sea salt. Continue simmering until the chickpeas are tender. Total cooking time should be no more than 45 minutes. Allow them to cool with the vegetables in their liquid.

## 12  Borlotti and cannellini

| | |
|---|---:|
| Dried beans | 1¼ cups |
| Baking soda | 2 tbsp |
| Garlic bulb | 1 |
| Tomato | 1 |
| Sage leaves | 3 tsp |
| Ex.v.olive oil | 2 tbsp |

Soak the beans overnight in cold water with the baking soda.

Cut the garlic bulb in half (don't peel). Drain the beans, rinse well and put in a saucepan with the tomato, sage, and garlic. Cover with cold water, bring to a boil, removing the froth from the surface. Reduce the heat, add the olive oil and simmer for 30-45 minutes. When the beans are very tender, remove from heat and let cool in the liquid. Season.

# Italian pantry

This is a basic list of pantry items that you will find useful when using *Italian Easy: Recipes from the London River Cafe*. Included are items that keep in the pantry for up to six months, and also everyday fresh ingredients to stock up on once a week and keep in the refrigerator.

We suggest always keeping canned tomatoes, and for quick soups good-quality canned cannellini and borlotti beans. Essentials to keep in the bottom of the refrigerator are red onions, celery, garlic, and a few fresh herbs, such as flat-leaf parsley and basil in season.

Choose an olive oil for cooking, and an extra virgin single estate oil for bruschettas, soups, and drizzling.

## Pantry

sea salt
black peppercorns
dried red chiles
bay leaves (fresh or dried)
dried oregano
fennel seeds
nutmeg (whole)
bouillon cubes/granules

capers
anchovies
black olives
extra virgin olive oil
red wine vinegar
aged balsamic vinegar
white wine
red wine
dijon mustard

canned tomatoes
cannellini beans
chickpeas
borlotti beans
dried porcini
lentils (Puy or Casteluccio)

all-purpose flour
semolina flour
risotto rice
polenta (cornmeal)
spaghetti
tagliatelle
short pasta

70% chocolate
blanched whole almonds

## Refrigerator

unsalted butter
crème fraîche
parmesan cheese
free-range organic eggs
pancetta

garlic
red onions
celery
flat-leaf parsley
sage
basil
thyme
marjoram

# Suppliers

A.G. Ferrari Foods
Imported Italian delicacies
To find retail locations
(in northern California only)
or place a mail order:
877-878-2783
www.agferrari.com
Customer Service:
14234 Catalina Street
San Leandro, CA 94577

Agricultural Marketing
Service (USDA)
To find a local farmer's
market in your area:
www.ams.usda.gov/
farmersmarkets/map.htm

Ai due Catini d'Oro sas
di Zecchin Rino e Co
Mustard essence
Piazza dei Frutti, 46
35122 Padova, Italy
1 39 49 8750623

Arthur Avenue Specialties
Fresh mozzarella, pancetta,
prosciutto, cotechino
sausage, anchovies in sea
salt, dried porcini
Mail Order:
www.arthuravespecialties.com
Customer Service:
34 Winans Drive
Yonkers, NY 10701
914-923-8115

Browne Trading Company
Fresh fish, seafood,
organic sea salt
Retail Market:
Merrill's Wharf
262 Commercial Street
Portland, ME 04101
207-775-7560, or
800-944-7848 (mail order)
www.browne-trading.com

ChefShop.com
Bottarga, salted anchovies,
olive oil, baking chocolate,
and other gourmet
specialty products
Mail Order:
877-337-2491
www.chefshop.com
Customer Service:
P.O. Box 3488
Seattle, WA 98114-3488

Chocosphere
Gourmet chocolates from
around the world, including
Valrhona, El Rey, Amedei,
and Green & Black's
Mail Order:
877-99-CHOCO (24626)
www.chocosphere.com
Customer Service:
P.O. Box 2237
Tualatin, OR 97062

D'Artagnan
Organic game and poultry
Mail Order:
800-327-8246
www.dartagnan.com
Customer Service:
280 Wilson Avenue
Newark, NJ 07105

D'Italia, Inc.
Italian gourmet food
specialties
Mail Order:
888-260-2192
www.ditalia.com
Customer Service:
1401 South Boyle
St. Louis, MO 63110

Dean & Deluca
Specialty foods and
premium wines
To locate retail locations or
place a mail order:
www.dean-deluca.com
Customer Service:
2526 East 36th Street
North Circle
Wichita, KS 67219
877-826-9246

Diamond Organics
Organic produce, eggs,
meat, pork, poultry, fish,
and pantry items
Mail Order:
P.O. Box 2159
Freedom, CA 95019
888-ORGANIC (674-2642)
www.diamondorganics.com

Esperya
Bottarga, prosciutto,
organic Pecorino, olive oil,
balsamic vinegar, pasta,
rice, lentils
Mail Order:
877-907-2525
www.esperya.com
Customer Service:
1715 West Farms Road
Bronx, NY 10460

Formaggio Kitchen
Casteluccio lentils,
imported dry pasta,
organic specialty flours
and polenta, olive oil,
artisan cheeses, mostarda
(mustard fruits)
Retail Locations:
244 Huron Avenue
Cambridge, MA 02138
617-354-4750
and
268 Shawmut Avenue
Boston, MA 02118
617-350-6996
Mail Order:
888-212-3224
www.formaggiokitchen.com

Igourmet.com
Gourmet meats (including
cotechino sausage),
cheeses, and specialty food
items
Mail Order:
www.igourmet.com
Customer Service:
1735 Front Street
Yorktown Heights, NY 10598
877-446-8763

Melissa's.
World Variety Produce, Inc.
Specialty produce available
in select retail locations
and via mail order
Customer Service:
P.O. Box 21127
Los Angeles, CA 90021
800-588-0151
www.melissas.com

Niman Ranch
Premium quality,
hormone-free beef, pork,
and lamb available in
select retail locations and
via mail order
Customer Service:
1025 East 12th Street
Oakland, CA 94606
510-808-0340
www.nimanranch.com

Piccinini Brothers
Prime meat, poultry,
and game
Retail Shop:
Tartare
653 Ninth Avenue
New York NY 10036
212-333-5300
Customer Service:
633 Ninth Avenue
New York, NY 10036
212-581-7731

Royal Rose Direct /
European Vegetable
Specialties Farms, Inc.
Cavolo nero, radicchio,
puntarelle
Mail Order:
www.royalrosedirect.com
Customer Service:
1120 Growers Street
Salinas, CA 93901
831-758-1957

Todaro Bros. Specialty
Foods
Imported olive oils, meats,
cheeses (including fresh
buffalo mozzarella),
confections, condiments
Retail Shop
Customer Service:
555 Second Avenue
New York, NY 10016
212-532-0633, or
877-472-2767 (mail order)
www.todarobros.com

Zingerman's
Olive oil, vinegar, fresh
bread, cheese, and other
traditionally-made foods
Mail Order:
620 Phoenix Drive
Ann Arbor, MI 48108
888-636-8162
www.zingermans.com

# Index

**The authors would like to thank:** Editor **Lesley McOwan** Recipe Editor **Susan Fleming** Designer **David Eldridge** Artworker **Marisa Sebastian** Editorial Assistants **Sue Birtwistle, Lucy Boyd, Jan Dalley, Ian Heide** Additional Photographers **Jeremy Hudson, Gary Calton,** Chefs **Theo Randall, April Bloomfield, Sian Wyn-Owen, Matthew Armistead, Joanne Wilkinson, Joseph Trivelli, Stephen Beadle, Felicity Southwell, Theodore Hill, Jan Gillies, Helio Fenerich** All staff **past and present at the River Cafe** & **Vashti Armit, Ossie Gray, Lynsey Hird, Charles Pullan, Ed Victor,** Richard Rogers, and David MacIlwaine.